Museum
Librarianship

Museum
Librarianship

Edited by
John C. Larsen

Library Professional Publications
1985

First published as a Library Professional Publication,
an imprint of The Shoe String Press, Inc.,
Hamden, Connecticut 06514

Printed in the United States of America

Library of Congress Cataloging in Publication Data
　　　Main entry under title:
　　　Museum librarianship.
　　　　　Bibliography: p.
　　　　　Includes index.
　　　　　　1. Museum libraries.　　2. Library science.
　　　I. Larsen, John C., 1927–
Z675.M94M87　　　1985　　　　　026'.069　　　　　85–10212
ISBN 0-208-01906-5
ISBN 0-208-01907-3 (pbk.)

This book is dedicated to the memory of
Dr. Gerd Muehsam
whose idea it was and who began the work.

Contents

Preface

This manual is intended to assist the museum librarian. It will also be useful to the museum director, administrator, curator, or trustee who is considering the establishment of a museum library or who wishes to examine the library functions of a given institution. It is general in nature, with no attempt to treat museum librarianship by type of museum. There is no discussion of differences between libraries in art museums and libraries in natural history museums, or between science museum libraries and history museum libraries. This is because basic principles, activities, and procedures remain the same, no matter what the subject specialization of the museum.

The manual provides fundamental background in all areas of library service for the newcomer to the museum library world, although it is to be hoped that such a person will have had professional library training. Perhaps the manual will be of greatest assistance to the librarian in a small museum library. In large libraries with many librarians, the cataloging librarian does not perform public service, and the preservation specialist does not select new books, but in the majority of museum libraries, one person, with clerical help, must assume the full range of operational responsibilities.

Each chapter of the manual has been written by an experienced museum librarian with expertise in the area discussed. The authors, who represent a variety of United States and Canadian institutions, are aware that in any museum library an unusual problem may arise. When this happens, imagination and common sense are needed to provide a solution. Often the librarian will find that a telephone call or personal visit to a similar library suggests a successful resolution.

This manual reflects current practice, and we hope that its publication will spur the formulation of guidelines and basic standards for museum libraries. It is noteworthy that *Standards for Art Libraries and Fine Arts Slide Collections* has been published recently by the Art Libraries Society of North America (Tucson, 1984), but no overall guidelines or standards for museum libraries have been developed up to the present time. The official museum literature concerned with standards for museum accreditation, published by the American Association of Museums (AAM), is silent on the subject of museum libraries. Interestingly enough, however, the confidential evaluations that precede the accreditation visits from the AAM do ask questions about the institution's library, but the quality of that library—or whether indeed there is one—apparently has little bearing on accreditation decisions, except in the case of museums that are considered to be research institutions.*

Finally, the editor wishes to acknowledge the advice and encouragement of Daphne C. Roloff, formerly Director of Libraries at the Art Institute of Chicago and presently Librarian at the Centre Canadien d'Architecture, throughout the preparation of this book.

John C. Larsen
December 1984

---

*Conversation with Patricia Williams, accreditation office of the AAM, 6 December 1984.

Introduction

William B. Walker

Museums have a universal appeal. Collections of objects, artifacts, specimens, or documents, systematically presented, tell us something about ourselves, our fellows, or the world around us. When suitably arranged and identified, these things may merely instruct us, or they may delight us as well. Museum collections may be small and specialized, or large and encyclopedic. If one's interest is not caught by a museum of fine arts or a presidential birthplace, then there is a museum of science and industry or a baseball hall of fame. There are, in short, museums for every field of knowledge – art, history, science, technology, and combinations of these – and they range from a small, one-room collection to a complex installation that may fill several city blocks.

According to the *Official Museum Directory 1983*, the American Association of Museums has identified approximately six thousand museums in the United States and Canada. Many are independent organizations existing on income from endowments and membership fees, some are governmentally supported, and others are departments in larger institutions, e.g., universities or corporations.

Perception of a museum is generally based upon the public aspects of its activities, its exhibits especially, but also its lectures, gallery tours, publications, films, and television programs. As every museum employee knows, these are the end products of the work that engages the staff in every type of museum. The objects, specimens, and artifacts must be collected, cataloged, and preserved before they can be exhibited (or placed in a study-storage collection) and interpreted through publications or lectures.

An ideal museum collection, regardless of its size or its nature, has been intelligently and sensitively selected, authoritatively cataloged, scientifically preserved and housed, and displayed and interpreted with intelligence and appeal. These activities cannot take place without a well educated, thoroughly trained, and currently informed museum staff.

All of this is prologue to the argument that within every museum there must be a library. Clearly, the nature of that library will depend upon the nature of the museum and its resources. The larger and more complex the museum, the greater are the demands upon its library—or libraries. The activities of a museum require the support of a library, no matter how small the institution.

The museum library is one branch of the family of special libraries. Like other special libraries, museum libraries tailor their collections and services to one or more special groups of users. They organize the collections according to the particular needs of these users. Museum library collections often include materials in special forms: photographs and slides, ephemeral publications (which must be regarded as having permanent value), publications in odd and oversize formats, and a variety of "nonpublications," such as manuscripts, memorabilia, realia, and other hard-to-organize forms.

In other ways museum libraries have much in common with other types of libraries. It is necessary to consider the special qualities or needs of museum libraries within the larger context of librarianship, so that every wheel need not be reinvented. There exist well-tested solutions to many of the problems encountered by the fledgling museum librarian. Some are peculiar to museum libraries; others are common to many libraries.

This manual will be most helpful to the librarian in a smaller museum, or in a new museum that does not have a well-developed library program. It is intended to answer some of the questions that the librarian will raise and to direct the librarian to the larger body of literature that supports the discipline.

When does one decide to establish a library within a museum? M. Noël Balke, in her contribution to this manual, writes that "the impetus to start a museum library develops when materials appropriate for a library collection exist in sufficient number within the museum to require organization to make them accessible." That usually comes early in the life of most museums, when the miscellaneous, unorganized book and catalog collections have outgrown the allotted shelves in the office of the curator or director, and retrieval of needed material has become difficult or impossible.

The decision to establish a library requires serious commitment of the museum administration and its trustees if an effective library is to be developed. The issues that must be addressed in implementing a library program are reviewed in the chapters that follow. They include such matters as: building the library collection and its physical facility, staffing the library with suitable personnel, organizing and preserving the collection, and serving the library's (and museum's) clientele effectively. The place of the library within the museum administration is discussed. The authors of this manual represent the broad field of museum librarianship, cutting across all subjects and types of museums. They are all practicing museum librarians who have brought their experience to this forum.

In the chapters that follow, a number of themes or motifs recur, viewed from differing angles by their respective authors. Among the major points are: (1) The relation of the museum library and its service to each of the traditional activities of the museum; (2) The place of the museum librarian within the museum administration as peer of, and coworker with, the curator and educator; (3) The primary and secondary constituencies of the museum library, i.e., the importance of service not only to the museum staff but also to museum members and other members of the larger community in which the museum is found; and (4) The determination of the mission of the museum library in light of the mission of the parent organization.

The establishment and maintenance of a good library in a museum is not an inexpensive undertaking, but strength in this central facility undergirds all the activities in the museum. The essential support that a museum library provides must be taken into full account when a museum reviews the effectiveness (cost- or otherwise) of its various departments.

Many modern museums pride themselves in their use of the latest techniques and equipment in their exhibitions and public programs. Modern techniques in the museum library, such as automation, are now well developed and used increasingly in American and Canadian libraries. It is hoped that this manual will guide the librarian and museum administrator in the judicious use of new techniques as well as the best of traditional museum library practices.

1 The Library and Its Parent Organization

Juanita M. Toupin

Today a library can be found in nearly every museum, regardless of size or type. Whether the museum is concerned with science, art, history, or the performing arts, its library closely reflects the historical development of the institution to which it belongs. While museums and libraries can trace their origin to the beginning of Western civilization,[1] public awareness of them as an educative force within the community is a recent development brought about by the profound social changes and modern technologies of the past decades. In planning the future of museums, Richard McLanathan, former president of the American Association of Museums, warns

> that public demands, and our obligations to meet them, will increase rather than diminish; that we must face not only the issues of today but also anticipate those of tomorrow; that, with the concept of continuing education, our role is significantly enlarged; that new standards of accountability that go with public funding are accompanied by broader notions of accountability to a broader public. That, in short, there are no more ivory towers, that museums must finally be where they should be, in the agora, not on the outskirts of life.[2]

All museums, regardless of size, wealth, or founding date, have a common aim. They seek to present the objects in their collections

1

in accordance with the best professional practice, thereby contributing to public knowledge and enrichment. To achieve this, museums have developed various supportive units, among which the library is one of the most important. The need for a good museum library has been clearly expressed in a UNESCO statement.

> Identification of the specimens coming into a museum calls in the first place for an expert staff and in the second for a good library of reference books, if the requirements of serious students are to be met. From this it follows that a museum must have a good reference library with all the standard works dealing with the subjects in the collections.[3]

The primary purpose of the museum library then, is to provide the information, published or unpublished, which enables curators and other museum personnel to carry on the tasks of researching, exhibiting, teaching, publishing, and interpreting the museum's collection for its public. The activities of museum personnel determine the functions of the museum library; in this it is like any other special library. The museum library, however, may also serve the public.

Management and Organization

The management and organization of the museum library should be entrusted to a trained professional librarian qualified to undertake these tasks. In a small museum, the librarian is directly responsible to the director, and in a medium-sized or large museum, to the administrator in charge of curatorial affairs. (See Tables 1 and 2.) As a professional, the librarian should have parity with other museum professional staff. A study by the National Endowment for the Arts defined professional staff positions in museums as "those requiring specialized training or experience."[4] Another source speaks of "personnel such as curators, librarians, designers, lecturers."[5] The administrative responsibilities of the librarian toward the various library collections are comparable to those of the curator toward museum objects. The library should be a separate department within the museum at the same administrative level as other comparable departments.

2

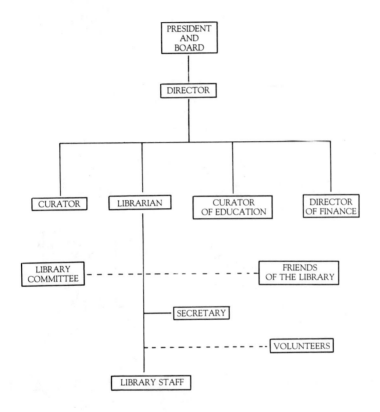

Table 1
Library in a small museum

3

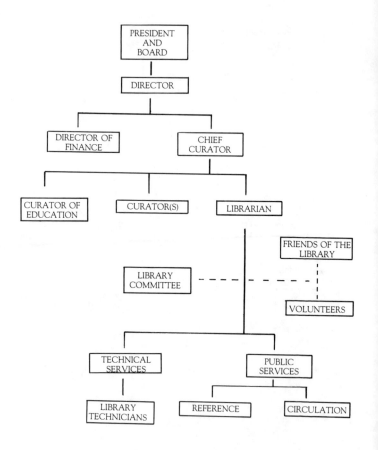

Table 2
Library in a medium-sized or large museum

4

The museum library can effectively fulfill its role only if it is recognized and supported by the museum administration, which must feel assured that the library's objectives and services are being properly maintained. The library must be provided with the financial and physical means to meet the requirements of collection development and maintenance, effective facilities and equipment, qualified staff, and promotion of library use and services. If the museum has a handbook of organization, the organization chart therein will indicate the position of the library in the structure, and the librarian's principal duties will be outlined. In museums without an organizational handbook, it is advantageous for the librarian to prepare an outline of library activities and duties, with a description of each, and to obtain approval of these by the museum administration. Such a document will minimize sources of confict with the administration and other department heads.

In administering the library, the librarian is involved with the museum director or deputy director, the curatorial departments, business officers, and committees. The librarian should establish a good working relationship with each department of the museum, although the daily work will bring the librarian in closest contact with those staff members (curators, educators, public relations personnel, designers, and restorers) whose activities require the services of the library regularly. Good communications are essential in day-to-day operations to achieve and maintain a high level of performance.

Promoting the Library

The librarian must take every opportunity to let the general public and the museum staff know what resources are to be found in the library, and how and by whom they can be used. Even in a small library where the librarian is his own public relations officer, this is an important activity. Information about the library can be presented in an attractive leaflet or small brochure which can be made readily available to every new museum staff member and library user. This publication may briefly state the aims and objectives of the library, describe the collections, indicate the library services available (photocopying, interlibrary loans, reference guidance, tours, etc.), and outline lending policies.

The basis for all library activity is adequate financial support. Much of the vitality and quality of the services the library performs is contingent upon adequate means. The finances of the library are of course closely linked with the financial situation of the institution. In the last twenty years museum funding has undergone tremendous changes. To meet mounting operating costs, museums today rely heavily on government and public funding to augment revenues, gifts, membership subscriptions, and private endowments. A recent survey published by the United States government shows that more than 50 percent of American museums are governed by private non-profit organizations, 36 percent by the government, and 10 percent by educational institutions.[6] The increase in public funding has affected many museum policies. Some museum libraries have had to waive earlier restrictions and make their facilities available to a broader public. As a result, they have become more involved in the community and are known to a larger, more diverse group of users.

The amount of funding allocated to the library depends upon the financial situation of the museum, the size of the library collection, and the extent of library services. The governing body of the museum, in determining the annual library budget, should always take into account the budget proposed by the librarian to ensure the services that the library is expected to provide, not only to the museum staff, but also to the public. A budget allocation sufficient to allow adequate staffing of the library is often overlooked.

The Library Committee and the Friends of the Library

The librarian may wish to have advisory assistance from persons not on the library staff. The most commonly utilized source is the library committee.

Many museum librarians have found it advisable to establish a library committee whose purpose is to work with the librarian in developing library services and increasing library usefulness. (The committee is always understood to be advisory only, and not administrative.) After receiving administrative approval for the establishment of such a committee, the librarian outlines the composition, method of appointment, terms of office, and duties of the committee in written form. Usually the museum board will want to appoint one of its members to the library committee to act as a liaison between the board and the committee. Others members of the committee may include the director of the museum or the deputy, curators, librarians and scholars from local academic institutions, museum patrons, collectors, and community leaders. Members should be selected carefully to avoid conflicts of interest and the committee should not be too large to manage. A five- to eight-person committee is typical. The librarian sits on the committee and often serves as secretary.

It is very important that committee members be genuinely interested in the development of the library. The librarian, too, must believe in the usefulness of the committee and be willing to share information about the library and its function in order to provide members with a working understanding of library matters.

A Friends of the Library group has a function which differs from that of the library committee. The function of the Friends of the Library is to enlist the support of persons in positions to be of genuine assistance to the library; and it is highly desirable that members be well educated in library matters and aware of library needs. They may be avid library users, retired scholars, or prominent society figures. Activities of the Friends of the Library may include assisting in acquiring archival materials and manuscripts of local artistic interest, raising money for library projects, soliciting gifts, and supplying volunteers for special activities. No activities, however, should be undertaken by the Friends without the approval of the librarian. The librarian should appreciative of Friends' efforts and should maintain good communication to enable the group to function effectively without undue interference in routine operational matters.

Administration of the Museum Library

Administrative organization has been defined by Floyd W. Reeves of the University of Chicago as "arrangement of the personnel for the accomplishment of the objectives for which the institution exists." Reeves adds that administrative organization "includes the division into groups of all those objectives . . . and allocation of such activities to individuals."[7] This statement could serve as a job description for present-day museum librarians.

The small museum library organizes its activities by function under the headings of administration, selection and acquisitions, technical services, and public services. Functions which do not fit into a departmental system, such as personnel, budgeting, accounting, and reporting, are normally considered to be the responsibilities of the librarian. These functions are basic in all libraries, regardless of size.

In a medium-sized or large museum where not only the staff, but the collection and the potential for growth are larger, library activities are more complex and require greater specialization in library work assignments and specific skills. As the library grows, new departments are established based upon the priorities of the library and the needs of its clientele.

Whether the museum library is small or large, an organization chart that represents the internal organization of the library is needed. In addition, each staff member should be provided with a procedure manual and an individual job description. The manual should indicate library policies and the duties of the various staff members. If there are no job descriptions for library staff members, it should be one of the first tasks of the librarian to prepare them for all staff members.

Administration is time-consuming and comprises the major activity of the librarian. The librarian in a small library, who may be the only professional staff member, must also assume the technical duties of the library, such as cataloging, classification, supervision of catalog card typing and filing, and preparation of library material for circulation, bindery, and repair. The librarian must be prepared to undertake anything necessary to the maintenance of good library service, but should of course be assisted by an adequate support staff.

Selection of library staff members is one of the most important responsibilities in library administration. In organizations large enough to have a personnel director, the librarian works through the personnel office, and in a smaller institution, through the director. In any museum library, the final decision and recommendation for

8

employment should be made by the librarian, who is in the best position to know where to find the best candidates, and also better able to judge the qualifications of a candidate in relation to a particular position and to the staff. The importance of hiring library personnel who meet the standards established by the professional library associations cannot be overstressed.

The librarian should be aware of current salaries offered in other museums and should make sure that library salaries equal those paid to other librarians as well as to professionals within the museum for work requiring similar education and skills. Professional organizations conduct frequent salary surveys which are published in library periodicals. These can be used by the librarian in discussion with museum administrators to upgrade positions and salaries.

A museum staff manual is invaluable to all new staff members for learning about the organization of the institution, major policies and procedures, personnel regulations, and general information about the various departments of the museum. New staff members should be made aware of the various codes of ethics that govern the conduct of professional librarians and museum workers, along with the ethics and professional practices prescribed within the museum itself.[8] Although the librarian should encourage application of the appropriate library standards, it must be recognized that certain administrative procedures affecting the library are governed by its parent organization and the specific museum regulations to which the library must conform.

The librarian prepares the annual budget, after carefully estimating the needs of the library to ensure sufficient funds for each budget item. This budget may be prepared unilaterally or submitted for discussion and approval to the library committee. After preparation, the budget is presented to the administration for final aproval.

Gifts and funds offered to the library are also administered by the librarian. Funds can often be obtained by applying for grants from foundations, agencies, or the government. Grant applications should be initiated by the librarian with the approval of the museum administration.

Selection and acquisition of material for the library demands the experience and skill of a professionally trained librarian working with the active collaboration of the curatorial staff and other museum specialists, such as educators, restorers, and designers. The acquisition procedures of ordering, receiving, budget control, and accounting require familiarity with the purchasing procedure of the institution, and the financial control required by the accounting department. In a small library, the actual processing of the orders, claims, and related correspondence may be handled by the librarian's secretary, and the new acquisitions are classified and cataloged by the librarian.

Clientele

The library's primary clientele is the museum staff, which may range in number from a few people to a large and interdisciplinary body, depending upon the size and diversity of the collections and upon the museum program of exhibitions and activities. The major responsibility of the library is to respond to the needs of these staff members, not only by having an efficiently organized collection and a judicious acquisition program, but also by being aware of the resources in other institutions and knowing where to locate information. The museum library is an active research center that interrelates with many other museum departments. It is especially concerned with the curatorial departments and those dealing with education, publications, and conservation, although it serves all agencies of the museum.

As a source of specialized materials documenting the museum's treasures and collections, the library is not only an asset to the museum but to the local community as well. Like its parent organization, the library has a vital educational role and its contribution can be felt in many spheres. To the general public, the museum librarian is usually more visible than the curator. The librarian is often the first person contacted when a visitor seeks information about the museum collections or activities.

Because of the range and depth of subject coverage in its collection of books, periodicals, and other materials, the museum library is frequently in a unique position to offer resources not duplicated in other institutions. Public libraries rely on museum library resources for information beyond the scope of their own collections. Secondary schools, colleges, and other teaching institutions also rely heavily on the specialized holdings of the museum library as well as on the various collections and artifacts in the museum to support adequately their degree granting program. Often libraries in academic institutions that maintain visual arts and art history departments do not duplicate the special materials found in the museum library (sales and exhibition catalogs, museum and scholarly journals, and specialized reference works) but depend on the museum library, formally or informally, to supply these. On occasion the museum library also serves readers and researchers beyond its immediate local area. It shares its resources with other institutions throughout the country by supplying its list of acquisitions to the union catalogs or to computerized databases.

The 1970s witnessed the arrival of the computer on the museum scene.[9] This technological development has significant practical implications for the museum library. It is now possible for museum libraries to join a state or national network (OCLC, RLIN, or others in the United States, and UTLAS in Canada) and to participate actively in shared programs. Computer terminals make the special resources of the museum library available to a larger audience than ever before, and conversely, a wider range of distant resources can be made available to the local patron.

Conclusion

Although museums have been in existence for a long time, they have only recently come of age in terms of organization and professionalism. It has been said that unknowingly the library organization and its professionals were models for the museum world. Daniel Robbins outlined the analogy between the two institutions in a recent working paper which pays tribute to the library organization and its concept. Robbins writes that

> despite the very real differences in the substance of the two activities, the appeal of the analogy remains very great, perhaps the most telling factor on museum training today. Its appeal is double: the effectiveness of its carrying of knowledge to the people was [John Cotton] Dana's spur; but the relative theoretical ease of its solution to the criteria of collecting, leading to a focusing on technical solutions to problems of storage, classification and delivery, remains the envy of art museums.[10]

NOTES

1. Germain Bazin, *The Museum Age* (New York: Universe Books, 1967), 14-15.
2. Richard McLanathan, "From the Director," *Museum News* 55 (January-February 1977):3.
3. *The Organization of Museums: Practical Advice* (Paris: UNESCO Press, 1974), 19.
4. National Endowment for the Arts, *Museums USA* (Washington: Government Printing Office, 1974), 84.
5. Council on Museums and Education in the Visual Arts, *The Art Museum as Educator* (Berkeley, Calif.: University of California Press, 1978), 600.
6. National Endowment for the Arts, *Museums USA* (Washington: Government Printing Office, 1974), 8-9.
7. Floyd W. Reeves, "Some General Principles of Administrative Organization," in Carleton B. Joeckel, ed., *Current Issues in Library Administration* (Chicago: University of Chicago Press, 1939), 1-21.
8. "Librarians' Code of Ethics," *American Libraries* 13 (October 1982): 595; Corporation des bibliothécaires professionels du Québec, *Code de déontologie* (Montréal: Corporation des bibliothécaires professionels du Québec, 1969); "Code of Ethics for Museum Workers," *Museum News* 52 (June 1974): 26-28; "Museum Ethics," *Museum News* 56 (March-April 1978): 21-30; Association of Art Museum Directors, *Professional Practices in Art Museums* (New York: American Association of Museum Directors, 1971).
9. Robert G. Chenhall, *Museum Cataloging in the Computer Age* (Nashville, Tenn.: American Association for State and Local History, 1975).
10. Canadian Museums Association, *2001: The Museum and the Canadian Public* (Ottawa: Canadian Museums Association, 1977): 86-91.

2 Staffing the Museum Library

Elizabeth Reuter Usher

As soon as the decision has been made by the museum administration to establish a library pertinent to the museum's collection, it
is advisable to hire a professional librarian. Together the administration and the librarian should formulate the purpose of the library
and determine its place in the organizational structure of the
museum. The extent of service to the public; the need for computerization of the important functions of acquisition, cataloging, and circulation; and the necessity or desirability of joining a bibliographic
network are fundamental questions to which the administration
should address itself at the time of the library's formation. It must
always be borne in mind that the basic purpose of a museum library
is to support the curatorial and other professional staff in its study of
the museum collections, and to provide research materials and
library assistance for museum exhibitions, lectures, and publications. The library plays a significant role in establishing the museum's
reputation as a research institution.

The museum administration and the librarian should jointly
determine basic library policy which, to avoid future misunder-
standing, must be in written form. The policy defines the scope of
the library collection and the types of materials to be collected and/
or housed in the library (e.g., books, microfilm, microfiche, slides,
photographs, original prints, films, recordings, and archival materials).

It sets goals for library service and indicates limitations on service, including the hours the library is open to the museum staff and the public. The policy must be reviewed as conditions change; any policy change may affect the staffing pattern. The size and type of staff (professional, paraprofessional, and other support personnel) needs careful study and planning because salaries make up the largest portion of the library budget.

Some museum libraries provide important community services. A museum library may be the community's principal library resource in its subject field, and may be required to serve a broad spectrum of users from the high school student to the advanced scholar. A university may enter into a cooperative agreement with a nearby museum to provide students with special access to the museum's library. Such services directly affect the staffing required.

Size and Type of Staff

The staff of a museum library should be of adequate size to perform efficiently the major functions of administration, collection development, acquisition, cataloging, reference, circulation, and maintenance. The smallest library requires a minimum of one professional librarian, plus support staff. As museum activities and the professional staff of the museum grow, use of the library increases and the need for additional research materials and library staff is a natural result.

Support staff for the professional librarian is of first consideration. Typing, filing, ordering, processing, retrieving, and shelving library materials are clerical and housekeeping chores necessary to the efficient functioning of a library. These routine tasks should be performed by support staff to free the librarian for the professional activities of administration, collection development, reference and research, and cataloging. As professional activities increase, additional professional staff will be needed. A ratio of 40 percent professional staff to 60 percent support staff has been recommended by the Art Libraries Society of North America as a standard for art museum library staffing.

14

If the administration is serious in its determination to establish a strong library that will support museum staff members in their research and give them access to other libraries' resources, it must provide *knowledgeable* library staffing. The librarian selected by the museum administration should have qualifications equal to those of other professional staff members who head museum departments. Equality of rank, status, and salary then becomes a foregone conclusion, and the stage is set for a good working relationship between librarian and fellow professionals.

The librarian must have the education and expertise necessary to select and provide research materials. A master's degree in library science from an accredited graduate library school is a necessity. With this degree the librarian is prepared to perform and direct the bibliographic and technical activities of a library. A strong academic background and a keen interest in the subject field in which the museum specializes are also essential. An advanced degree in the subject field may be a requirement where highly specialized bibliographies and other services are expected of the library staff. In addition, proficiency in at least two foreign languages is a prerequisite in most museum libraries.

While an excellent educational background is of primary importance, administrative experience and demonstrated management skills are also highly desirable. The librarian must know how to set up a library, prepare a budget, select and provide research materials, and be completely familiar with procedures and sources. Much of this knowledge comes only from experience.

It is important for the administration to consider personal qualifications in selecting a librarian. A high degree of intelligence, leadership ability, good judgment, imagination, initiative, and good health are necessary qualities. The librarian must have the ability to communicate clearly both verbally and in writing. An articulate librarian has a great advantage; the manner of presenting library needs can make the difference between approval and disapproval of financial and other support for the library. Patience, wisdom, integrity understanding, and good communication skills are prerequisites in the librarian's role as a member of the museum staff, whose members often work under great pressure with difficult time schedules. The librarian occupies a highly visible position both within the museum and on the outside, and the prestige of the museum is enhanced if the librarian, as one of its principal staff, makes a favorable impression.

Support Staff

The minimum support staff requirement for the library is a secretary/assistant, and this position should be in the library's budget. Excellent typing and filing skills and preferably a bachelor's degree are standard qualifications. A reading knowledge of a second language and an interest in the subject field of the museum are useful.

It is usually necessary to employ a stack attendant to retrieve and shelve materials and to maintain the library, i.e., dust books, keep stacks in order, etc. A minimum of a high school education should be required, although student help can sometimes be used advantageously for this work.

Participation in Professional Organizations

The administration should encourage the librarian to participate actively in professional organizations. Professional meetings, seminars, and publications can assist the librarian in providing knowledgeable service. Among the established professional library associations are the Special Libraries Association, the Art Libraries Society of North America (ARLIS/NA), and the American Library Association. The Special Libraries Association has particular relevance for museum librarians as it brings together librarians from all types of museums in its Museums, Arts & Humanities Division. The Art Libraries Society of North America has a "Museum TOL (Type of Library) Group" for art museum librarians. Subject-oriented organizations are also important. Among these are the American Society of Information Scientists, the Society for American Archaeology, the College Art Association, the

American Historical Association, the Society of American Archivists, and the Society of Architectural Historians.

Professional organizations are a source of continuing education as well as valuable resources for information and contacts. Personal contacts made by an intelligent librarian, active in appropriate associations, can increase the scope of resources available to the museum. If it is the policy of the museum to pay the professional association membership fees of other professional staff, the policy should include the librarian. A professional librarian who is enabled to think, plan and act at a professional level by good support staff will usually feel encouraged to take part in professional association activities.

Volunteers

Many museums rely on the services of volunteer help to staff their libraries. This is particularly true of smaller museums whose budgets are limited, but with escalating costs most larger museums now welcome volunteers in all areas, including the library. However, even in the small museum, unless there are extremely severe financial problems, it is advisable that the administrator of the library be a professional librarian and a permanent staff member. If this is not possible, a volunteer who is a professional librarian should be sought. Retired librarians are sometimes available and usually prove to be very competent. Unemployed recent graduates of accredited library schools often make excellent volunteers because of their interest in gaining work experience. It should be pointed out that volunteer staffing is a controversial issue, and there are recognized advantages and disadvantages.

Volunteers can be very helpful with clerical tasks and special projects. As a general rule, continuing duties should be reserved for regular staff since volunteers tend to work on an irregular schedule. In training volunteers, it is important to explain the functions of the library, its place in the organization, and its goals. The volunteer should be made to feel a real sense of responsibility toward the position and to recognize the importance of the contribution made to the library and to the museum as a whole. It is necessary that the museum administration, as well as the library director, acknowledge this contribution and express their appreciation.

Volunteers should never replace employees in regular jobs. They should be given work which will supplement that of the permanent staff—work which could not otherwise be done and which will enlarge the scope of library services. Because volunteers have the time, the desire to help, and often very good contacts with the media and community organizations, they can do excellent public relations for the library and often can bring in much-needed funding for special projects and programs. They are generally drawn from a high-income stratum, and they can influence their friends for the benefit of the museum. Sometimes they may even provide a reservoir of potential employees.

Each applicant for volunteer service should be asked to complete an application form. This makes it easier for the librarian to ascertain skills and other qualifications before interviewing prospective workers. Although most applicants for volunteer positions are willing to perform any assigned task, any restrictions as to assignments they will accept should be determined during the interview so that the librarian can make an intelligent decision about the suitability of the volunteer.

Time sheets of the hours worked by volunteers should be kept and, at least once a year, the volunteers should be thanked by letter for the service they have given to the library. Since tax deductions are allowed for transportation, lunch, and out-of-pocket expenses in connection with volunteer work, the thanks can be stated in such a way that the letters can be used by the volunteers for tax purposes.

Conclusion

The most important thing to remember in staffing the museum library is that it is the library staff, interacting with both materials and users, that creates the library program. A roomful of books and other documents, however fascinating, cannot make a full and dynamic contribution to museum staff or the public without competent professional library direction.

Ahrensfeld, Janet L.; Christianson, Elin B.; and King, David E. *Special Libriaries: A Guide for Management*. 2d ed. New York: Special Libraries Association, 1982.

Art Libraries Society of North America. "Standards for Staffing Art Libraries." *ARLIS/NA Newsletter* 5 (April 1977): suppl. 1–6.

Eggleton, Richard, issue ed. "Personnel Recruitment and Selection in the 1980s." *Drexel Library Quarterly* 17 (Summer 1981). Entire issue devoted to library staffing.

Flanagan, Leo N. "Some Second Thoughts on Survival in the Seventies; or Two Views of the Volunteer Dilemma." *Catholic Library World* 48 (October 1976):112–14.

Gibson, Robert W., ed. *The Special Library Role in Networks; A Conference Held at the General Motors Research Laboratories, Warren, Michigan, May 5–6, 1980*. New York: Special Libraries Association, 1980.

Jenkins, Harold. "Volunteers in the Future of Libraries." *Library Journal* 97 (15 April 1972):1399–1403.

Masling, Annette, ed. "Museum Volunteers—Friends or Foes?" *Art Documentation* 1 (Summer 1982):113–15.

Metropolitan Museum of Art. "*The Volunteer Programs at the Metropolitan Museum of Art*." New York: Education Services, Metropolitan Museum of Art, 1980.

Naquin, Mary M. "Creative Role of the Art Museum Volunteer in the United States." *Museum* 29, no. 1 (1977):19–20.

Newsome, Barbara Y., and Silver, Adele Z. "The Art Museum as Educator." In *The Museum Volunteer*. Berkeley, Calif.: University of California Press, 1978:241–55.

Rogers, Rutherford D., and Weber, David C. *University Library Administration*. New York: Wilson, 1971.

Trainer, Leslie. "METRO Workshop on Volunteers in Libraries Sparks Controversy, Offers Practical Advice." *American Libraries* 7 (December 1976):666–67.

Usher, Elizabeth R., and Weinberg, Valerie. "Volunteers in Libraries (bibliography)." *Art Documentation* 1 (December 1982):209–10.

Veaner, Allen B. "Librarians: The Next Generation." *Library Journal* 109 (1 April 1984):623–25.

Warner, Alice Sizer. "Voluntarism and Librarianship." *Library Journal* 97 (15 April 1972):1241–45.

Wriston, Barbara. "Museum Volunteers in the United States," *Museum* 29, no. 1 (1977):15–17.

3 Building Museum Library Collections

Katharine E. S. Donahue

Librarians in many different kinds of libraries over a period of many years generated an extensive body of literature on selecting library materials. The routines of acquisitions and processing which apply to all libraries are available in a number of handbooks. One excellent work is *Acquisitions Management and Collection Development in Libraries*. (See bibliography.)

This chapter will explore the differences that pertain to selection for museum libraries. The technical details do not differ from those that apply to other libraries, but the philosophy that guides selection of books and other materials relates directly to the purpose and goals of the parent institution. Like most other special libraries, the museum library is concerned primarily with the needs of its internal clientele — the museum staff.

Background for Selection

The dictionary defines *museum* as "an institution devoted to the procurement, care, and display of objects of lasting interest or value." To these purposes, most museums would add the research — scientific or historical — required for the preparation or documentation of exhibits. The museum library exists first and foremost to support the museum's varied functions.

Selecting materials and building a library collection are accomplished in relation to the museum's overall goals and the goals and and objectives of each of its programs. If the museum does not have a clearly articulated statement of priorities and goals, the astute professional librarian should be able to encourage museum officials to develop one so that the library may identify its own priorities and write an appropriate selection policy.

Intelligent selection requires an understanding of the museum's responsibilities for collections, displays and exhibits, and research. The librarian must learn a good deal about the objects the museum actively collects, the content of its present collections, and their strengths and weaknesses. The library, whether long established or newly developing, builds its collection to reflect and to contribute to the museum's purpose through a responsive and carefully planned acquisitions program.

Some analysis is in order: To whom is the library providing the most service? The least? How much time is devoted to the function of serving as a research facility for the curatorial staff? What are the responsibilities of the curators? Is the library involved in public programs such as outreach education? Does the library have collections of its own that require curatorial attention?

Museums support a variety of activities. They include curatorial research involving the care, arrangement, and documentation of collections (there may be curatorial research unrelated to the collections); public exhibits and displays of collections; educational programs for the public; and often some form of formal training for volunteers. A responsive library provides materials to support all of these activities.

Once the priorities of the museum are clearly identified, developing a balanced acquisitions program is relatively easy. If the museum emphasizes growth, care, and organization of its collections, the library responds by allocating an appropriate amount in its budget to support these activities. The library may develop a comprehensive collection in certain areas to support this activity within the constraints of budget and availability. If the museum places significant emphasis on outreach activities or education, the materials the library collects will be very different. Each museum activity requires that the library devise selection criteria for evaluating pertinent materials.

A selection policy has two purposes. First, it defines the subject areas in which the library acquires materials, and it states the library's responsibilities and procedures for acquisitions in those subject areas. Although the policy is drafted by the librarian, it should be developed in cooperation with and input from the professional staff members of the museum, and approved by the museum administration. It is recommended that the policy be reviewed annually and revised to reflect any changes that become desirable or necessary. Any policy is always subject to improvements dictated by experience in living with it, and of course any revisions in the policy should be approved by the administration. The result of matching the museum's subject areas with the library's collection is an acquisition profile to guide selection of material. If the profile is an accurate representation of the interests of the museum and the users of the library, the wasteful purchase of irrelevant materials can be avoided.

The second purpose of the policy is to provide a clear statement of the selection responsibilities and authority of the library. The policy identifies the library as the department of the museum responsible for acquiring books, journals, and other informational material as delineated in the policy. The policy should give the library total control of its own budget to prevent library monies from being encumbered without the knowledge or consent of the librarian. Without this control, a balanced acquisitions program that enables the library to serve its constituents effectively cannot be assured.

Budget

Although there are various ways to prepare a materials acquisition budget, the budget request process for the library would be expected to follow the format and procedures used by the parent institution. A budget request or outline should be prepared even if one is not required by the museum's administration. A starting point is an analysis of the monies expended for the various categories of material in the previous year — serials, reference books, monographs and materials in formats other than print. Most libraries request an increase in their budget allocations each year just to maintain the same level of service by keeping pace with rising costs; additional amounts will be required if the collection and the library's program are to be expanded. Requests for budget increases of both kinds should be accompanied by brief statements of justification. Statistics on the rising costs of books and journals are published periodically in *Publishers Weekly* and *Library Journal*. In addition to formal justification, curators and other professional members of the museum staff often can be persuasive advocates with the administration for library budget increases. They are, after all, the ones whose work will be hampered if the library cannot maintain and regularly add to an adequate collection of pertinent literature.

Many museums do not have budgets adequate to support any of their activities, and as a result all departments, including the library, are underfunded. But in any case, administrators must continually be made aware of the library's value to the museum. It may be that a competent librarian, as the museum's information specialist, can identify some special project grants available in the museum's areas of special interest. The librarian would want to make sure that wherever possible, any grant applications would request monies for materials needed to support the various aspects of the projects or programs.

A well-justified, well-documented budget request, although time-consuming to prepare, is worth all the time it takes. It should, for instance, contain some specific examples of ways in which the library and its staff have contributed to various museum projects during the past year, and helped curators to find needed information or to solve problems. For the museum librarian who is new to the job, preparing a budget request is an excellent opportunity to evaluate acquisition allotments and justify more adequate funding to support museum programs.

The budget request is of course what the librarian wants; it is a statement of professionally-perceived, required funding for the library. The budget allocation that is eventually received is the reality—what the museum's administration feels it can spend—and this is the firm budget figure from which purchase funds may be drawn. Sometimes when requesting funds for an expanded program or new projects, it is good strategy to present the plan broken down into phases and to request funds for one phase at a time. The administration can then see fully the planned project and its benefits to the museum, but have the opportunity to fund one phase at a time.

One of the most difficult factors in the acquisitions budget is usually the cost of subscriptions and standing orders. Before monies can be allocated for books or other materials, the costs of journals and irregular series must be ascertained as exactly as possible. Funds necessary for standing orders for irregular series must be estimated. Once subscription costs have been figured, the remainder of the selection budget is apportioned to cover essential reference works, museology literature, and materials in the subject areas of the museum.

Museum librarians with relatively fixed budgets often complain of their inability to maintain book-buying power because of steady erosion by the relentlessly increasing price of journals. Serial material, however, remains vital in museum libraries as the source of the most recent information in research fields. In the budget war between journals and books, most museum libraries agree that the serials must win.

Budget control is based on constantly current knowledge of how much money has already been spent and a careful estimate of how much will be required to pay for outstanding orders. The object is to spend all available monies in a fiscal year without overspending drastically. This can involve some adroit juggling toward the end of the fiscal year when, to use the acquisitions budget completely, the librarian orders more books than can be paid for under the current year's budget, knowing that some titles will not arrive until the new fiscal year begins. If more books than can be paid for arrive before the end of the fiscal year, it is only a matter of waiting a week or two before paying the invoices out of the new fiscal year's budget allotment.

A simple form of accounting should be utilized to keep track of encumbrances and expenditures. A ledger should be kept for each fiscal year, and an automated accounting system is a desirable alternative to manual bookkeeping. It is now feasible to use a personal computer or word processor for maintaining an accounting of acquisition funds.

Since budgets are rarely as robust as museum librarians might wish, it is often helpful to develop a cooperative acquisitions agreement, formal or informal, with an institution sharing similar collection interests. This can be especially significant in the purchase of an important but expensive work. One copy in the region may be sufficient if the item is available through cooperative access agreements.

Museum libraries acquire a wide variety of materials, such as, new and antiquarian books, journals, maps and charts, technical and research reports, catalogs, government publications, microforms, iconographic materials, manuscripts, and photographs. Materials are acquired in various ways; some are purchased, some are donated, and some are received through exchange programs. Other materials, such as archival items, are generated in the museum and transferred to the library when appropriate.

Each method of acquisition requires its own record-keeping procedures. In considering purchases, the librarian will need to develop a broad base of information concerning what is available in the field of interest to the museum. This means regular perusal of pertinent journals for reviews and advertisements of new book titles, and ensuring that publishers place the library on their mailing lists to receive announcements. Often members of the professional staff of the museum may be asked to serve as subject specialists, or even bibliographers, to assist in the selection of material. If the library is building a collection of both current and retrospective material, appropriate subject bibliographies are used as selection sources. Mail order booksellers are good sources of information about material currently in print. Antiquarian booksellers are sources for out-of-print materials; their subject catalogs are often good working bibliographies for collection building.

Annual meetings of such organizations as the American Library Association, Special Libraries Association, and the American Association of Museums are ideal places to increase the librarian's awareness of general sources and specific titles through personal contact with exhibitors at the extensive exhibits prepared for these events. Antiquarian bookfairs throughout the country are also good places for broadening one's knowledge of sources and materials. It is useful to keep an eye open for auctions and estate sales, since the owners of collections—some of them perhaps in the museum's areas of interest—often have valuable related reference books and other library materials. It is a good idea to remind members of the curatorial staff to find out whether there are related library materials available from the source when they buy objects or receive them as gifts to the museum.

Museum staff members who are involved in helping to build the library's collection are more apt to use it and take pride in it than those who are not.

The museum bookstore can be a valuable source of information about new titles. It may be possible to share the use (and the cost) of basic reference tools such as *Books in Print (BIP)* and *Publishers' Trade List Annual (PTLA)* with the bookstore.

In-print material may be ordered in several ways. Occasionally a cooperative administration may direct the museum bookstore to handle ordering of in-print books for the library. Under the best of circumstances, the bookstore may pass on to the library the bookseller's discount it receives from publishers.

A more usual source is the jobber, or library wholesaler. Jobbers handle all ordering procedures for in-print materials and bill accordingly. Whether use of a jobber is economical or even available as an option for the library depends upon the amount of material to be ordered and the administrative procedures of the institution. For example, some publicly funded museums must use a designated purchasing agent.

Another alternative is to order directly from the publisher or a bookseller. Before ordering a recently published book from a bookdealer's catalog, it is wise to check *Books in Print* for the publisher and the price. It may be less expensive to order directly from the publisher. (*BIP* provides the publisher's address.)

Journal or serial subscriptions may be placed directly with the publisher or through a subscription agency. Use of the agency, even with its fee, greatly facilitates the handling of subscriptions. Instead of fifty or one hundred orders and invoices, there is only one. The subscription agent will supply a subscription list or comprehensive invoice, and keep track of renewals and the status of the titles, making clerical tasks easier.

Standing orders for monographic series are usually best placed directly by the library, either with the publishing house, if it will accept standing orders, or with a jobber. A standing order insures receipt of valuable, but often very irregularly appearing parts of a series, although it makes budget allocation difficult because of the unpredictability of receipt. In some instances, it is possible to request that the publisher send a pro forma invoice (requesting advance payment) before actually mailing unusually expensive items on a standing order. This gives the library the option of accepting, postponing, or declining delivery of a particular title.

It is necessary to keep track of what materials are on order. A simple method is an "in process" file of all the material not yet received. The file is made up of forms, preferably 3" x 5" (available from library suppliers), one for each item ordered. If serials are not ordered through a subscription agent, each serial title will also have a form. Depending upon preference, one or two copies are sent to the vendor and one or two retained by the library. Filing order records under the title often makes material easy to locate, although some libraries file records under author. An order number on the form helps identify orders. An expeditious system should be developed to authorize payment of invoices by the museum business office.

Many libraries are members of a bibliographic network, such as OCLC (see Chapter 4). If the museum library is fortunate enough to be part of such a system, the acquisitions subsystem of the network is a viable alternative to an in-house manual system, but the costs and benefits must be carefully evaluated for each library.

Exchanges

Many museums maintain a publications program consisting of a scholarly and/or a popular series, including magazines. Besides their original purpose, these publications are also valuable to the museum library in another way—they form the basis of an exchange program.

Exchanges are an excellent, inexpensive way to increase the resources of the library. They are publications exchanged between institutions sharing a similar purpose. The essentially "free" publications received are incorporated in the library just as if they had been purchased. Theoretically, the publications exchanged are of like monetary value, have an equivalent number of pages, and are desired by both institutions. Some exchanges, especially those with a foreign institution, may seem unbalanced in favor of American and Canadian libraries in terms of the relative value of material exchanged. This is especially true of institutions in countries with stringent currency regulations; they have money to publish materials, but find it difficult or impossible to send money out of the country to purchase American or Canadian publications. Under these circumstances foreign institutions are usually eager to participate in an exchange program which relieves the library of the cost and paperwork involved in purchasing subscriptions in foreign funds.

Once established, exchanges become almost self-perpetuating and are often easy to forget because of their sporadic appearance. Establishing exchanges should be the prerogative of the museum library, in collaboration with the curatorial staff and the publications editor of the museum. Publications outside the scope of the library collection should not be accepted.

Exchanges are initiated by writing to an institution that publishes one or more series desired for the library. When agreement has been reached on the titles each participant will send, each institution places the other on its mailing list to receive those titles. Although exchange programs require minimal maintenance, an occasional review is advisable to verify that the expected publications are being received and that they continue to be pertinent.

Exchanges can be very time-consuming for the library, as publications must be prepared for mailing (stuffing, addressing, and metering). These labor-intensive tasks are very suitable for a team of volunteers. The direct costs of an exchange program (overrun printing costs, packing materials, postage, time) should be considered before one is started. The benefits of an exchange program usually more than compensate for the time and labor invested, and can prove one of the most cost-effective programs of the library. Furthermore, some of the material received in exchange may be obtainable in no other way.

Exchange material can also be obtained from gift and exchange departments in university libraries. The departments often distribute lists of duplicate books and journals from their collections. The material is usually free except for the price of postage.

Archives

Archival materials produced by a museum include correspondence, publicity releases, reports, budgets, papers, grant proposals, photographs, plans, artwork, and any other records generated by the museum staff in the performance of their work. If the library is responsible for acquiring and caring for all the disparate archival material produced by the museum, an archival policy must be agreed to and understood by all staff members of the museum. The policy establishes which materials belong to the museum, and which belong to the staff member who created them.

The success of an archival collecting program depends upon the cooperation of the entire museum staff. All staff members must be encouraged when discarding files and other records to call the librarian, who will make decisions concerning retention of the material. This presupposes that the museum librarian is knowledgeable about archival practices and the philosophy of the museum, and points up yet another aspect of the work requiring professional qualifications.

Gifts

The museum librarian should impress upon the rest of the museum staff that the library must have the final decision about accepting gift books and other library material. All gift material is evaluated for its contribution to the existing collection, subject to the criteria in the selection policy, like any other material. Does the material provide new information or does it duplicate items already available? If a number of items are offered, will the donor consider giving only the material that is not already in the library? If an entire collection is accepted, written consent that all duplicate or inappropriate material may be disposed of by the library should be secured from the donor.

Gifts, which should not be accepted unthinkingly, can be a valuable source of titles that would otherwise be unobtainable or unaffordable. The library should encourage, and even solicit, appropriate gifts which have no strings attached.

Current United States tax laws permit donations of money, securities, books, equipment, and other items of value to recognized nonprofit [501(c)(3)] institutions to be tax deductible. To claim this tax deduction, the donor or an appraiser retained by the donor must establish a fair market value acceptable to the Internal Revenue Service. It is inappropriate for the recipient institution to evaluate donations it receives, as this could be construed as a self-serving conflict of interest. It is, however, the responsibility of the accepting library to make sure that gift material has not been accepted at an inflated value.

This means that the librarian must be knowledgeable about current market values.

The librarian must understand the museum's accessioning and deaccessioning policies, with special attention to the potential difficulties in accepting unwanted items. The kind of documentation needed for a gift of library materials is dependent upon the policies of the museum registrar, as is the procedure for acknowledging gifts. In any case, a letter of acknowledgment from the library to the donor is appropriate, and often a bookplate identifying the donor is attached to each item.

Friends of the Library

Most museums have a friends group or support group dedicated to helping the museum by raising money and/or providing volunteer help. It is appropriate for the library to seek support from this group, perhaps even encouraging the organization of a special subgroup or separate group dedicated to the library. If friends group funds (raised for this purpose) are distributed among divisions or departments of the museum, it is the librarian's responsibility to justify the inclusion of the library in the allocation.

Grants

Obtaining grants from extramural agencies for specific acquisition projects should never be overlooked as a source of additional funds Preparation of a grant proposal requires work, but it can be a valuable process because it forces the librarian to compile important statistics and documentation about the collection that frequently prove useful for other purposes. It can also be an exercise in creativity and requires valuable interaction with other members of the museum staff. Grant proposals require analysis of the strengths and weaknesses of the collection and justification for enriching a particular area of the collection.

Selecting a potential funding agency involves research into the many possible public and private sources of funds at local, regional, and national levels. After identifying the agency most likely to provide financial support, the actual format of the grant proposal must always conform to the specifications of the given agency. Foundation and government agency program staffs are usually very glad to hold preliminary discussions about possible projects and provide guidance in making applications.

Other Sources of Financial Support

Methods of raising money for purchase of library material depend upon the policies of the museum. For example, the library may be allowed to retain photocopying and photographic fees. If the museum is private, the library may charge for the use of its resources; there may be one fee schedule for individuals and another for corporate users. Periodic sales of duplicate and irrelevant items (selection policy notwithstanding, this material always seem to accumulate), perhaps incorporating additional material donated especially for the event, may prove valuable both as a source of revenue and of public awareness and support.

Conclusion

The need for the library to be involved in the broad spectrum of museum affairs and its activities cannot be stressed too strongly. The librarian must know not only the library and its collections, but those of the museum as a whole; the curators and their areas of work and research; and the exhibits being planned by the museum. Integration and application of this knowledge is fundamental in developing the acquisitions policy and program appropriate for the library and the museum it serves.

Annual Register of Grant Support, 1983–1984. 17th ed. Chicago: Marquis Professional Publications, 1982.

Collins, Marcia R., and Anderson, Linda M. *Libraries for Small Museums.* 3d ed. Columbia, Mo.: Museum of Anthropology, University of Missouri-Columbia, 1977.

Feeley, Jennifer. "Museum Studies Shelf List." *Museums Studies Journal* 1 (Spring 1983):i–xvi.

_____. "Museum Studies Shelf List: Additions and Updates." *Museum Studies Journal* 1 (Spring 1984):55–59.

Ford, Stephen. *The Acquisition of Library Materials.* rev. ed. Chicago: American Library Association, 1978.

Foundation Directory. 8th ed. New York: Foundation Center, 1981.

Futas, Elizabeth, ed. *Library Acquisitions Policies and Procedures.* 2d ed. Phoenix, Ariz.: Oryx Press, 1984.

Magrill, Rose Mary, and Hickey, Doralyn J. *Acquisitions Management and Collection Development in Libraries.* Chicago: American Library Association, 1984.

Niles, Judith. "Acquisitions Fund Accounting on a Word Processor." *Library Hi Tech* 1 (Fall 1983):10–13.

Osborn, Andrew D. *Serial Publications: Their Place and Treatment in Libraries.* 3d ed. Chicago: American Library Association, 1980.

Ratner, Rhoda S., and Monkhouse, Valerie, eds. *The Role of the Library in a Museum.* Boston: American Association of Museums / Canadian Museums Association, 1980. Available from the Smithsonian Institution, Washington, D.C. and the National Museums of Canada, Ottawa, Ontario.

Schwartz, Carole, and Bain, Alan L. *1984 Information Packet.* Chicago: Museum Archives Task Force, Society of American Archivists, 1984.

4 Organizing the Collection

Sylva C. Baker

Whether the museum owns a one-shelf collection of books or one that fills many shelves, a collection is not a library unless it is arranged in a systematic manner and the contents are made accessible by means of a catalog. The challenge of organizing a museum library is to arrange both print and nonprint materials and to describe their contents in a manner which enables users to retrieve needed information. Just as the purpose of the museum library is to support museum activities, the responsibility of the museum library cataloger is to understand the informational needs of the museum staff. The cataloger facilitates retrieval of information by providing access points to materials related to the institution's collection, its history, administration, exhibitions, and research. Fortunately for the museum librarian, every curator deals with organizing and cataloging a collection of some kind and the librarian will find much more understanding among the curatorial staff for the cataloging needs and methods of the library than will most librarians with other clienteles.

Types of Catalogs

The organization of the library should permit the user, to paraphrase the classic description by Charles A. Cutter, to identify and locate material by author, title, or subject. The means to that goal is the catalog, which can take a variety of formats: book, COM (computer output microfiche), computerized, or card. In selecting the most suitable format, the following criteria should be considered: flexibility in adding or deleting titles and making corrections; the number of users who can search the catalog simultaneously; security of the catalog from loss, damage, or disorder; and cost.

A book catalog format provides the advantages of portability, compactness, and multiple copies. The disadvantages are inflexibility in making changes and poor security. Additions, corrections, or deletions must be added to each copy of a book catalog or enumerated in a supplementary volume. Supplements are inconvenient as they require readers to search in several volumes. Frequent printing of a book catalog to correct this problem adds to the cost of the cataloging process. Lack of security results in torn and missing pages or the disappearance of entire volumes from the library.

Microfiche catalogs, sometimes called COM, have become popular in the last ten years. Although cataloging information must be stored on magnetic tape to produce a microfiche catalog, once that is accomplished, microfiche is inexpensive to produce and reproduce, permitting frequent updating and multiple copies. Fiches are portable and take up little space. However, each time a title is added to the collection, all the records have to be resorted. When the catalog becomes large, the necessary resorting of the catalog requires much costly computer time, although this is not a burden for collections with less than fifty thousand titles. The principal disadvantages are the need for an adequate number of functioning machine-readers for catalog users and the lack of public enthusiasm for reading the video screens. Like all mechanical systems, the microfiche catalog is dependent upon an electrical power supply and equipment that works properly.

The computerized catalog is the most flexible form of library catalog; it is the simplest and fastest to update. Microcomputers are available at prices that are not beyond the reach of a small library. Libraries with a collection small enough to be stored on a disk and with a limited number of users might well consider a computerized catalog. The essential determinants are:

1. storage space for database and program. Considering the growth rate of the collection, how long will the

microcomputer storage space be adequate? Will funds be available to permit necessary expansion?

2. the number of terminals needed to permit access to users within a reasonable waiting time. Users include the technical processing and reference staff as well as other library users.

3. the cost of large storage space and multi-terminals and the annual maintenance costs of hardware and software. A sizeable annual budget may be required.

4. backup disks or tapes as protection from loss or erasure. Backup records are a necessary security measure. The computer program should be designed to prevent un-authorized tampering with records; a password system should be considered.

Many museums are currently using in-house mini- or mainframe computers or have access to large machines. The possibility of storing and retrieving records on these larger systems by means of a terminal located in the library should be explored.

The traditional card catalog can meet all the requirements of a museum library, large or small. Its records are easily revised, useable by many readers simultaneously (the needed cards will not all be in the same drawer), not easily lost, and not dependent upon mechanical equipment. It is unlikely that the card catalog will ever be "down."

An alphabetically arranged dictionary catalog in which cards for author, title, and subjects are interfiled is entirely adequate for the majority of museum libraries. The major cost, after the initial outlay for furniture and space, is the budget commitment for staff time, card production, and filing.

Cataloging Print Materials

The cataloging principles discussed in this section are based upon use of the card catalog, but apply to other formats as well.

The catalog card is the vehicle for information that describes print or nonprint material and indicates its location in the library. The *Anglo-American Cataloguing Rules* (AACR2) and library literature abound with discussions of the definitions and rules of descriptive and subject cataloging applicable to the museum library and will not be reviewed in detail. The museum library has special needs and as the introduction to *AACR2* recommends, special libraries should "use the rules as the basis of their cataloging and augment their provisions as necessary."

Basically, each book will have cards for its author(s), title, series, subjects, and the shelf list record. The shelf list, which contains cards arranged by call number, should be kept near the technical processing area and away from the public catalog if possible. The shelf list provides an inventory of the books in the order in which they are shelved.

The essential elements of descriptive cataloging are: author(s), title, compiler/editor/illustrator/translator, edition, place of publication, publisher, data, paging, illustrative material, notes, and tracings. They can be as detailed as needed. Simple cataloging needs only author, title, edition, publisher, date, paging, statement of illustrations without descriptions or number, and subject headings. Few notes and tracings for illustrators, translators, and ancillary contributors are needed. The level of cataloging offered by the Library of Congress Cataloging in Publication (CIP) program exemplifies adequate simple cataloging. If additional facts and greater detail are important to the museum staff and other library users, cataloging and tracing should be more extensive. For libraries where the book as an object is important, e.g., historical societies and rare book collections, descriptive cataloging should be detailed, indicating the variations in each edition and supplying all needed notes. If the information content of a book is important for users, subject cataloging can be more extensive.

Often the specialized needs of museum library users are best served by added entries which go beyond the subject headings supplied in standard lists (see *Subject Cataloging* below). Both books and periodicals may be involved. Additional access points often used are authors associated with the museum (staff, donors, volunteers, and others who have published books, journal articles, chapters of a book, pamphlets, contributions to an anthology, or reviews) and pertinent historical material (books and articles about persons or events significant to the museum's history, collection, exhibitions, expeditions, auctions, sales, visitors, etc.).

The traditional practice of assigning and recording an accession number for each volume acquired by a library is not necessary for museum libraries. Books are adequately identified by call number and the acquisition information (order number, vendor, price, and date of arrival) penciled on the page following the title page along the inner margin. Duplicate copies may be indicated by "Copy 2" following the call number. The staff time expended in maintaining an accession numbering system is of little value for libraries that acquire few multiple copies.

Classification of Books

Each book in the library receives a unique call number for identification. The first element of the call number is a classification number that identifies the subject of the book, its placement on the shelf, and its subject relationship to the books shelved around it. The classification number can indicate geographical location, historical period, zoological and botanical families, etc.; there are specific tables for these notations in both the Library of Congress (LC) and Dewey Decimal (DDC) classifications. The second element of the call number is the book number (or author number or Cutter number). It is composed of letters and numbers representing the main entry of the book, which is usually the name of the author (individual or corporate) but can be the title when authorship is not definitive. The book number keeps books on the same subject together in alphabetical order by author. A decimal numbering sequence permits insertion of main entries while maintaining the alphabetical order. Cutter tables are needed for assigning book numbers when original cataloging is done by the library.

The two major systems for arranging books by subject are the Library of Congress and Dewey Decimal classifications. The Universal Decimal Classification (UDC) is popular in European museums, but is little used in the United States and Canada. Some museum libraries have developed unique classification or location systems. Unique systems raise procedural difficulties if the library joins a shared cataloging system or purchases prepared catalog copy. Museum library catalogers sometimes complain that DDC is too broad to address in-depth subject collections adequately; others object to the LC arrangement of subject matter. Although these may be valid complaints, a standardized classification system has the most advantages: utilization of the CIP information found in books, availability of prepared catalog cards without the cost of customizing, availability of LC catalog cards, and ease of participation in bibliographic networks or shared cataloging programs.

Library of Congress classification is recommended for museum libraries which acquire extensively in their subject fields. Regularly used in academic libraries, most museum library users are accustomed to working with it. The full classification is available from the Library of Congress, but only those schedules that relate to the library's collection, e.g., "N" for visual art, "Q" for science, "T" for technology, etc., need be purchased. All libraries should purchase the "A" (general works and museology) and "Z" (library science and bibliography) schedules, however.

In addition to classification schedules, catalog cards and subject heading lists can be purchased from the Cataloging Distribution Service of the Library of Congress. It should be noted that the Library of Congress offers the convenience of payment through a deposit account. The museum library can deposit a sum of money with the Library of Congress against which purchases are charged, replenishing the account when necessary. Information about establishing an account and payment procedure can be obtained from the Cataloging Distribution Service, Library of Congress, Washington, D.C. 20541.

The Dewey Decimal Classification is used widely by public and school libraries. It is adequate for a museum with a small, basic collection, but libraries owning many titles on a single subject may be forced to use awkwardly long call numbers.

Whether LC or DDC is used, books not shelved with others on the same subject because of size, format, or inclusion in a special collection should be given a location symbol as part of the call number. "R" or "Ref" for Reference Collection, "Bro" for Browsing, "F" for Folio, and "SP" for Special Collection are often used. This indicator is usually placed immediately below (or above) the call number. For example, the call number

QL
461
.N5
.S78
F

would be found in the folio section of the library. Location indicators for materials other than books are usually placed above the call number. To facilitate inventory, a separate shelf list is maintained for materials in special shelving sections.

Periodicals

Museum libraries develop a periodical collection to provide current information for readers. The size of the collection depends upon the research needs of the museum. Whether obtained by purchase, exchange, or gift, periodicals sometimes prove difficult because of changes in title, numbering system, size, and format; in addition, publication may cease without notice.

Each periodical received should be represented in the public catalog by entries for title, sponsoring agency (if appropriate), and subject. If there is a title change, a new set of cards referring to all previous titles is entered in the catalog. The original card set remains in place with the date of the final issue and reference to the new title added. This is necessary to trace the history of the periodical title.

In addition to an entry in the public catalog, a separate visible (Kardex) file of periodical titles should be maintained in the technical processing area to record the receipt of each issue. The public catalog informs the reader if the periodical title is kept, but the visible file indicates the holdings of individual issues. Public catalog entries for periodicals should be stamped "see visible file" to direct readers.

In a Kardex file, two 4" x 6" cards for each periodical title are stored back to back. (The cards can be purchased from any library supply company.) The top card is designed to record the receipt of each issue. A monthly check of the visible file will reveal those periodicals which have not arrived on time. It is necessary to claim missing issues from the publisher or subscription agent within three to six months after the date of issue. After that time, many publishers disclaim responsibility.

The bottom card of the pair is preprinted to record payment of subscriptions: time period, volume number, invoice or purchase order number, date, and amount paid. It is advisable to record the number of the agent's or publisher's invoice when payment is made. In making claims for missing issues, the vendor frequently requests the invoice on which the serial was billed.

For a modest periodical collection (fewer than two hundred titles), a microcomputer is an ideal "catalog" for serial holdings. It can handle checking in, making and keeping track of claims, and recording changes in serial titles. Printouts of the periodical collection can be circulated to staff to provide a convenient record of the library's holdings. A copy of the printout can be kept in the reading area for quick reference, and copies can be exchanged with other libraries as a first step in library cooperation. Periodical vendors and bibliographic networks offer computerized programs for checking in serial publications, but the cost effectiveness is questionable for a small collection.

There are two ways to arrange the library's periodical collection. Periodicals can be classified with appropriate call numbers and intershelved with monographs and other materials on the same subject. The other method is to arrange them alphabetically by title on shelves separate from the monographs. The disadvantage of intershelving monographs and periodicals is the unequal rate of growth between the two types of material. Periodical collections grow more rapidly than those of monographs and each title requires shelf space for expansion. When periodicals are alphabetically arranged, a problem arises if a change of title separates older issues of a periodical from current issues. Probably the most satisfactory practice is to classify and shelve periodicals in call number order in a separate section of the bookstacks with adequate room for expansion. With this arrangement, even if there are title changes, the call number is unchanged and all issues of each periodical remain together.

Subject Cataloging

The two standard subject heading lists, *Sears List of Subject Headings* and *Library of Congress Subject Headings (LCSH)*, are appropriate for museum libraries. The *Sears List*, a modified version of *LCSH*, is adequate for a small museum library, but *LCSH* is recommended for the detailed subdivisions of subjects required by museum libraries. Individual institutions have prepared specialized subject heading lists for research collections. An example is the subject heading list published by the Peabody Museum of Archaeology and Ethnology at Harvard University. Creating an individualized subject list or thesaurus is a monumental undertaking, but many museum libraries supplement the standard heading lists with subject entries applicable to their own collections.

If the museum library plans to purchase catalog cards from the Library of Congress, commercial vendors, or online shared cataloging systems, *LCSH* should be adopted because Library of Congress headings are used by these systems. Use of a nonstandard list of headings requires extensive editing, revision, and authority file work to maintain consistency and few libraries can afford the necessary amount of staff time.

Additions to and modifications of subject heading entries are recommended to provide access points of interest to the museum's clientele. To assure consistency throughout the catalog, an authority file is maintained to indicate the library's preferred entry for names, organizations, special subject headings, or other entries for which there are variants in spelling or use. The authority file is a file drawer of cards which list the standard forms of entry for persons, organizations, places, and objects represented in the library catalog. The file includes variant spellings with "see" and "see also" references to the form of entry used by the library. The librarian often must select the standard form for foreign names, organizations known by initials, and pseudonymous authors. Publications which use a variant spelling as title should be cataloged under the form of entry chosen by the library. A "see" card that refers the reader to the standard entry should be placed in the public catalog where the variant spelling would normally be entered.

As an example, if *Linnaeus, Carl* is the standard entry selected by a library, additional cards would be filed for *Linne, Carl von*; *Linnaeus, Carolus*; and *Von Linnaeus, Carl*, each stating "See Linnaeus, Carl." In the authority file, the entry for *Linnaeus, Carl* would list the possible variant spellings with a "see from" (x) reference:

> *Linnaeus, Carl*
> > x Linne, Carl Von
> > x Linnaeus, Carolus
> > x Von Linnaeus, Carl

The authority card for "see from" references leads from the forms of entry not used to the form used. The "see also from" (xx) reference leads to related subjects which are entries in their own right:

Herbicides
　x Weed Killers
　xx Pesticides
　xx Agent Orange
　xx Fungicide

The example above indicates that there is no entry in the library catalog for "weed killers" and that "herbicides" is the heading under which information on weed killers may be found. The cross reference cards in the public catalog would be:

Weed Killers	Pesticides
see	see also
Herbicides	Herbicides
	Poisons
	Spraying

Maintaining both a separate authority file and "see" and "see also" references in the public catalog is highly recommended, but in small libraries with limited staff and time, the use of cross references in the catalog only can be a reasonably effective working solution.

Entries in the authority file should indicate the "authoritative" publication or source from which the selected form of entry was taken. The *National Union Catalog*, Online Computer Library Center (OCLC), *LCSH*, *Who's Who in America*, and the *Cumulative Book Index* are frequently used as authorities. An advantage of using *LCSH* is that the *LCSH* volumes become, in effect, a subject authority file. The use of OCLC as an authority guarantees that the library catalog will be consistent with *AACR2*.

Preparation of Catalog Cards

As noted earlier, sets of Library of Congress catalog cards for each book acquired by the museum library can be purchased from the Library of Congress Cataloging Distribution Service. Each set includes a main entry card, shelf list card, and unit cards. Suggested LC and DDC call numbers are provided on the cards in the descriptive cataloging immediately below the tracings. The upper left corner is blank to permit the individual library to type its own call number on the cards. A separate unit card for each traced heading is prepared.

The advantage of Library of Congress cards is the ability to obtain descriptive and subject cataloging information without searching. This technique is known as cataloging with copy. However, LC cards can be modified by the museum library. Subject headings that are not used can be deleted from the main entry cards and notes can be typed in. Alternate subject headings and added entries can be utilized to meet the needs of the museum catalog and its users.

Original cataloging is very time consuming, and the number of bibliographic tools needed to research and prepare original catalog copy represents a major financial investment in tools and staff time for a library. Acquisition of a basic collection of these tools as well as annual supplements and successive editions is not cost effective for a small library which purchases trade publications almost exclusively. Larger museum libraries do, however, frequently acquire material that has not been cataloged on LC cards. Because report and pamphlet literature, exhibition catalogs, organization yearbooks, and directories do not always receive LC card production, the museum library must be prepared to undertake original cataloging where the source for the catalog copy is the document itself.

In the library which acquires fewer than three hundred titles per year, preparing simple original cataloging using the document as the copy source is not difficult. Main entry cards (with call number) for several titles are typed on a single sheet of card stock that is photocopied to provide the necessary number of cards for the catalog. Appropriate headings are typed across the top of the cards before filing. If a microcomputer is available, the museum librarian should review the available programs for cataloging and investigate use of a printer to produce cards.

Preparation of catalog cards is extensively described in Hopkinson (1977), Collins and Anderson (1977), Bloomberg and Evans (1981), and Miller and Terwillegar (1983).

Bibliographic Networks

The card production facilities of cooperative online cataloging systems such as Online Computer Library Center (OCLC), Research

Library Information Network (RLIN), Washington Library Network (WLN), and the University of Toronto Library Automation System (UTLAS), are changing the typography of the catalog card. Although there have been complaints about the appearance of computer produced cards, there have been none about the speed of acquiring them. Catalogers in museum libraries that are members of bibliographic systems can use a terminal to search for information about a title they wish to catalog. When the catalog record appears on the screen, it is reviewed for suitability. All the variable fields for call number, title, series, author(s), subject headings, added entries, and local notes may be edited by the librarian.

After the catalog record on the screen has been changed to meet the needs of the library, a "produce" command brings a set of cards to the library within five to seven days. The cards bear full cataloging as requested, including call numbers in the left upper corner, location indicators, local notes, and tracings printed across the top—all in alphabetical order ready for filing. At the same time, the library's acquisition was recorded in the central database of the network from which a tape can be extracted to produce an in-house online catalog when the library acquires the computer capability.

This convenience is costly. Membership costs, system services, telecommunication time, and equipment services may cost a minimum of $4000 per year *excluding* the initial cost of the hardware and installation, fees for cataloging, producing cards, and mailing them to the museum library. The cost-benefit ratio for joining a bibliographic utility may be worthwhile if a library catalogs at least one thousand titles per year. Libraries acquiring fewer than one thousand titles can sometimes utilize the services of a bibliographic system through a "piggyback" or cooperative membership. The networks differ in their definition of and means of handling less than full membership status. If a neighboring library makes less than full time use of its terminal, sharing a membership and terminal costs should be explored.

Nonprint materials

Nonprint materials acquired by museum libraries include manuscript collections, graphics (prints, photographs, etc.), maps, audiovisuals, original art, realia, and other three-dimensional items. Each nonprint medium has technical details that should be included in cataloging in addition to the standard statements of authorship or responsibility, artist, producer, publisher, etc. For example, among pictorial materials, cataloging of films should note millimeter size, number of reels, and whether sound or silent and black-and-white or color. Photographs, prints, maps, and phonograph recordings have different technical features. For each nonprint item, the content is recorded, and the location in the library is noted, usually above the call number. Nonprint materials of the same format are usually kept together rather than intershelved with books to allow efficient utilization of shelving or other appropriate housing. A separate shelf list of nonprint material is maintained.

With the advent of laser disks, video cassettes, computer software, and constantly evolving technological devices, the museum librarian must remain alert to developments in cataloging procedures. *AACR2* provides the most complete rules for standardized cataloging of nonprint materials. Hopkinson (1977), Bowditch (1975), and Betz (1982) supply detailed instructions for handling audiovisuals, photographs, and graphic materials.

Binding

Binding periodicals (and rebinding books) is part of collection organization and maintenance. Although small museum libraries may not keep periodicals permanently, usually museum libraries preserve periodicals in bound volumes to protect individual issues from loss or damage.

Most museum libraries use the services of a commercial bindery. Before entrusting any material to the bindery, the librarian should thoroughly discuss the library's requirements with a bindery representative. Clearly establishing the specific services desired is important.

Binderies offer a variety of bindings from which the librarian must choose with regard to the way in which they will be used. Sewn bindings are strongest and most expensive, and are preferred for permanence. In binding (and rebinding) page margins are always reduced, and if the inner (gutter) margins are narrow, part of the text may disappear. Sewn bindings often keep the book from lying flat for photocopying. Adhesive bindings, which are improving in quality, lie flat, preserve margins, and cost less, but allow pages to become detached if the volume is used roughly or frequently.

Procedures for preparing library materials for binding should be standardized, and each item must carry its own instructions. When preparing journals, careful collation is required to assure that the issues in each volume are in numerical order and their covers retained. The number of lines needed for the spine title and whether the title is to be printed vertically or horizontally should be indicated in the instructions. Each serial should have a binding color that is used for all its volumes; white spine lettering has the greatest visibility.

Additional information on binding can be found in Chapter 5.

Weeding the Collection

When library materials become irreparably damaged, superseded by newer items, or divergent from the criteria set forth in the selection policy (see Chapter 3), they may be permanently withdrawn from the collection. After the decision to withdraw an item has been made, it is necessary to remove all cards pertaining to it from the catalog and shelf list. If the catalog is computerized, the record must be deleted from the database. The end papers or title page of the withdrawn material should be stamped "Library Discard" with the name of the library to show that it is not a lost or stolen item.

Conclusion

It is abundantly evident from a reading of this chapter that the organization of the museum library collection is an almost constant process of choices and decisions including: what kind of a catalog will be most efficient in providing access for the library's users; which cataloging system to use; and decisions about periodicals and bindings. There is no one best decision for all libraries and the right decisions will depend upon the thoughtful analysis of the given situation.

Berman, Sanford. "Do-It-Yourself Subject Cataloging: Sources and Tools." Tools." *Library Journal* 107 (15 April 1982):785–86.

Betz, Elizabeth W. *Graphic Materials: Rules for Describing Original Items and Historical Collections.* Washington, D.C.: Library of Congress, 1982.

Bloomberg, Marty, and Evans, Edward G. *Introduction to Technical Services for Library Technicians.* 4th ed. Littleton, Colo.: Libraries Unlimited, 1981.

Bowditch, George. *Cataloging Photographs: A Procedure for Small Collections.* rev. ed. Nashville, Tenn.: American Association for State and Local History, 1975. (Technical Leaflet 57)

Collins, Marcia R., and Anderson, Linda M. *Libraries for Small Museums.* 3d ed. Columbia, Mo.: Museum of Anthropology, University of Missouri-Columbia, 1977.

Dowell, Arlene Taylor. "Subject Headings." In *Cataloging with Copy*, Littleton, Colo.: Libraries Unlimited, 1976. Pp. 111–34.

Godden, Irene P., ed. *Library Technical Services: Operations and Management.* Orlando, Fla.: Academic Press, 1984.

Hopkinson, Shirley L. *Descriptive Cataloging of Library Materials.* 5th ed. San Jose, Calif.: Claremont House, 1977.

Library of Congress Subject Headings. 9th ed. 2 vols. Washington, D.C.: Library of Congress, 1980. Quarterly and annual supplements.

Malinconico, S. Michael. "Catalogs & Cataloging: Innocent Pleasures and Enduring Controversies." *Library Journal* 109 (15 June 1984): 1210–13.

Maxwell, Margaret F. *Handbook for AACR2: Explaining and Illustrating Anglo-American Cataloguing Rules Second Edition.* Chicago: American Library Association, 1981, [1980].

Miller, Rosalind E., and Terwillegar, Janice C. *Commonsense Cataloging: A Cataloger's Manual.* 3d ed. New York: H. W. Wilson, 1983.

Nielsen, Brian. "An Unfolding, Not an Unveiling: Creating an Online Public Library." *Library Journal* 109 (15 June 1984):1214–18.

Reynolds, Dennis. "Cooperative Group Membership in OCLC." *Special Libraries* 73 (January 1982):27–32.

Sears List of Subject Headings. 12th ed. New York: H. W. Wilson, 1982.

Sheridan, Wendy. "AACR2 and Graphic Materials: Use for a Descriptive Catalog in a Science Museum." *Art Library Journal* 6 (Winter 1981): 13–33.

5 Preserving and Maintaining Museum Library Collections

Nina J. Root

Preserving and maintaining museum library collections is an extensive topic that is difficult to present in one chapter. For museum professionals, the responsibility to preserve older materials in the library collection is as great as that of acquiring the current materials relied upon by scientists, curators, artists, restorers, designers, historians, and other museum professional staff members. Collections take many forms in a museum library, and often include such nontraditional materials as museum memorabilia, archives, records of exhibits, artifacts, and works of art. Museum librarians are expected to maintain and preserve these diverse collections.

The deterioration and even destruction of library books, archives, manuscripts, photographs, films, recordings, and microforms has reached staggering proportions; maintenance and preservation grow increasingly complex as new information formats, such as computer tapes and video discs, appear. Deterioration is not restricted solely to older materials; modern paper and bindings are deteriorating at faster rates than those of books published in the sixteenth century. Studies show that over 90 percent of the books published between 1900 and 1939 will not survive to the year 2000 and that clothbound books published today will not survive for fifty years.[1] Modern archives and manuscripts are yellowing, microfilm is drying out, color slides are fading, motion pictures from the 1920s and 1930s are crumbling to dust, leather bindings are disintegrating, and pages mended with cellophane tape are discoloring. It is regrettable that over the years libraries have not had sufficient funds and staff to preserve collections, and that air-conditioning was not always available. Today librarians face the tasks of rescuing badly decayed collections and preserving current materials.

Gloomy as the picture is, preventive and restorative measures can nonetheless be taken. Preservation of the collection should be an integral part of the museum library's overall acquisition and service policy. Maintenance is an important aspect of preservation; when library materials are properly housed and well cared for, the rate of deterioration is slowed. Even in underfunded and understaffed libraries that cannot rebind, restore, or microfilm their collections, a well thought-out, *written* preservation program with a statement of policies and procedures is necessary. If every staff member is familiar with the program, selective action can be undertaken as problems arise. The written program should include statements on housing the collections; housekeeping; shelving; protection from mutilation, theft, fire, and flood; emergency disaster procedures; and policies and procedures for physical processing, binding, mending, preservation, and restoration.

Housing the Collection

Housing is one of the first lines of defense in preserving a collection. When materials are maintained in equipment designed to protect and support them, wear and tear are lessened. Although a great variety of library storage equipment is on the market today, equipment to house odd-sized or oddly-shaped materials is not always readily available, and alternative equipment may have to be utilized. Catalogs of industrial, warehouse, laboratory, or school equipment, office furniture and supplies, and store furnishings often contain equipment that can house odd-sized materials. Sometimes imagination is all that is required to recognize the potential of an unfamiliar rack or case.

Most stack shelving is made of steel covered with smooth baked enamel to prevent abrasion of bindings and chemical interaction with paper, glue, and bindings. The need for end panels and protective overhead canopies to prevent dust accumulation should be assessed. Stacks should be well ventilated to prevent mildew, and the height of shelving should be considered. In closed stacks where only library employees retrieve and shelve books, high stacks (up to seven feet) can be used. In open stacks, six feet is the maximum height because users may drop books when removing them from the top shelves, and in re-shelving, may force them in at random, damaging adjacent books. Users should never reshelve books. Providing stations throughout the stacks to hold books for reshelving by library personnel not only avoids misshelving, but also prevents damage.

Folio and thick volumes present a special shelving problem. Ideally, no book over 18" or 20" high or with a spine wider than 3" is shelved upright because the weight of the volume warps covers, separates pages from the binding, and weakens the spine. Extrawide shelving is needed to allow folio and thick volumes to be laid flat. Large, heavy volumes should not be placed on top shelves because dropping them causes great damage. Designating bottom shelves for large volumes avoids the problem and simplifies removal and reshelving. If folio shelving is not available for large volumes, standard double-faced metal shelving, without braces between the two sides of the range, can be easily adapted. Standard steel shelves placed at the same level on both sides of the range allow volumes as high as 34" and as wide as 24" to be laid flat. Placing the shelves a few inches apart vertically uses space economically.

Folio shelving can also be used for maps, broadsides, paintings, architectural drawings, and large illustrations. Large paper materials should never be rolled or folded if map or architectural drawing cases are not available. All items housed on open shelving should be protected with acid-free folders or wrappers.

Unbound journals should not be shelved issue by issue; when the time comes for binding, covers will have become torn, indexes lost, edges frayed, and issues missing. It is preferable to shelve unbound issues of journals on sloped display shelving with storage space beneath for previous issues. Unbound issues can also be placed in Princeton files or pamphlet boxes. A policy of binding journals as soon as a volume is complete prevents their loss and damage.

Manuscripts, autographs, archives, and ephemera are subject to the same deterioration problems as other paper materials, with the additional concerns of ink and typewriter ribbon. These materials should be placed in acid-free folders and stored in manuscript boxes or file cabinets of the proper size. They should never be bound or folded because binding fosters contamination of nonacid paper by its acidic neighbor, and folding breaks the fiber of the paper and causes irreversible damage.

Film-based materials (photographs, slides, reels of film, and microforms) also present housing problems. To prevent adverse chemical reactions, all film is stored in metal equipment with a baked enamel surface. Under no circumstances should nitrate film be kept in the library; it is highly flammable, subject to spontaneous combustion, and gives off a gas that is dangerous to humans and animals, and contaminates other films. Nitrate film should be converted to safety film, but if for some reason archival nitrate film must be retained, the advice of a knowledgeable film conservator should be sought. Motion picture film is stored in metal containers and stacked flat, no more than two or three reels high. Photographs are placed in individual acid-free protective envelopes, mylar sleeves or folders, and housed in boxes or files of suitable size. Photographic negatives are kept in individual acid-free envelopes in dark, dry storage areas. Color slides need to be protected from heat, light, moisture, and pollutants by storing them in inert plastic sleeves, baked enamel metal boxes, or specially designed slide cabinets and trays; original slides should be placed in cold storage. Microfilms are stored in metal boxes with air vents or in acid-free envelopes and are housed in baked enamel metal files.

It is essential that the equipment used for viewing film-based materials be kept in perfect working order, with light bulbs of correct wattage and clean, unscratched lenses. Staff and patrons must be trained to operate the equipment correctly.

Recordings and tapes must be kept from direct sunlight and heat. Records are stored upright in acid-free sleeves, with sufficient support to prevent leaning and warping. Tapes are stored in acid-free boxes with the reels in an upright position; they should not be stacked. Baked enamel steel shelves are recommended.

Special collections of rare books or other materials should be housed separately in a protected area. If possible, rare books should be shelved in bookcases with doors that can be locked to keep out dust and browsers. Fragile books and bindings are placed in special boxes, cases, or wrappers; items bound with metal studs and clasps should be housed similarly to protect adjacent materials.

Environment

Much has been written about the effects of environment on living creatures. Inanimate objects are also affected by pollution, light, humidity and temperature. Housing library materials in an unsatisfactory environment leads to deterioration and destruction. Optimum humidity and temperature for various library materials are as follows:

Material	Optimum humidity (%)	Optimum temperature (°F)
Books and paper	50–55	65–68
Microforms	40–45	65–68
Motion picture film	40–50	65
(in archival storage)	25–30	0
Photographs	40–50	65–68
(in archival storage)	25–30	0
Recordings and tapes	55	65–68
Slides	40–50	65–68
(in archival storage)	25–30	0

Since it is difficult, if not impossible, to provide a different environment for each type of library material, a constant temperature of 68°F and a constant relative humidity of 50 percent is recommended. Fluctuating temperature and humidity are equally deleterious to the stability and health of library collections. The chemicals and dust that pollute the atmosphere interact chemically with paper, film, leather, and cloth to cause extensive damage to library collections. Light, particularly ultraviolet rays, from sun and lamps is extremely harmful to library materials. Air-conditioning is the most reliable environmental control available today. In libraries that are not air-conditioned, turning off radiators in the winter can help control excessive heat. A dehumidifier that draws water out of the air helps control moisture in humid areas, and containers of water placed on radiators and sills are beneficial in arid areas. During the summer, large fans that circulate air help prevent mildew.

Lights should be turned off in stack areas and left on only in main aisles. Windows should be shaded, or covered with a specially treated film through which ultraviolet rays cannot penetrate. Fluorescent lighting, which emits a high level of ultraviolet rays, should be modified by filters available from electric supply companies.

Air conditioner filters must be cleaned at regular intervals to keep dust and pollution down. Windows that must be opened for ventilation should be fitted with dust particle filtering screens which must also be cleaned regularly. Dust filtering screens are available in large hardware stores. The blades of electric fans accumulate dust that can be blown throughout the library when the fan is used; the fan blades and the wire blade cover must be kept dusted and clean.

Housekeeping and Security

The details of housing and housekeeping may seem endless, but they must be attended to in order to preserve collections. Simple requirements, such as keeping the stacks, shelves, and bookcases neat and dusted, and having the floors swept, dry mopped or vacuumed regularly are vital to the health of the collection. Wet mopping and liquid waxing are not recommended because wet mops may spatter water or wax on books placed on lower shelves, and the chemicals used in washing and waxing floors may cause irreparable damage. Books should be dusted or vacuumed by a trained, reliable technician because loose or brittle pages and pieces of bindings can be sucked into the cleaner or broken off by rough dusting. The cleaning staff should dust shelves and books with feather dusters or with dust cloths to which some dusting spray had been applied.

Silverfish, mice, roaches, and other destructive pests are fond of establishing residence in libraries, but regular visits from a capable exterminator will evict such squatters. Liquids and sprays should never be used because they discolor and damage books; powders and pellets should be used instead. An infestation of bookworms or beetles

56

requires a professional exterminator. Improper treatment by unskilled hands can destroy library materials faster than insects.

Fire is an obvious threat to library collections, but a sprinkler system can cause more damage than flames and smoke. Some museum libraries have installed gaseous-chemical fire extinguishing systems, but they are very expensive. Less costly smoke detection systems react to heat and smoke and provide the staff with the time to carry out evacuation procedures and to utilize fire extinguishers. Common portable fire extinguishers contain either water- or chemical-based solutions that may harm books, but it is better to damage the books in a small area than to have a fire spread or a sprinkler system wet down an entire stack. The best safeguards against fire are periodic inspections of all wiring, prohibition of smoking in the stacks, and segregation of any library process that involves flammable materials. Fire drills for the evacuation of the library and notification of fire and emergency squads should be practiced regularly. Emergency telephone numbers should be prominently posted throughout the library.

Water damage is a serious hazard to library materials, whether from sprinkler systems, burst pipes, or the elements; piping should be checked regularly and all windows should be caulked. A procedure should be devised for removal of threatened materials if a leak occurs. Damage can be minimized if the staff is trained to handle emergencies. Water-damaged books should be fanned out with clean, absorbent paper placed between the leaves and left to dry for several days in a well-ventilated area. When dry, they should be inspected for mildew. Mildew can be halted by placing the books in a freezer for several days. Dried books should be cleaned and placed in a book press. Books caked with mud should not be cleaned until they are completely dry. Peter Waters's *Procedures for Salvage of Water-Damaged Library Materials* provides a full description of necessary and proper procedures.

Although security systems to prevent theft and vandalism are relatively inexpensive to maintain, the initial installation is expensive. With or without a security system, the exits from the library must always be controlled. Entrance doors into the library and into areas containing special collections should be sturdy and have strong locks that cannot be easily picked. There are inexpensive alarms that can be installed on doors to infrequently used collections. The number of keys distributed to staff members should be strictly controlled; members of the library staff should be made responsibile for the security of their colleagues and the library collections. The museum security service should be asked to assist in a survey of library security and must be made aware of the value and importance of the library collections.

Proper shelving procedures are especially important in maintenance. Pages and shelvers must be carefully trained to handle books correctly and taught that there is more to shelf work than mere "re-shelving." Shelvers should straighten the book collection by pulling books forward to the edge of the shelf, pushing protruding volumes back, and shifting books to the left to eliminate leaning. On shelves that are not completely filled, book supports or book ends high enough to hold books upright should be used. The supports should have smooth edges that will not scratch books or shelves. If a library does not have enough book supports, bricks wrapped in acid-free paper make a good substitute.

Tightly packed shelves should be relieved by shifting volumes to the shelf above or below. When bays or ranges threaten to become over-crowded, the space situation should be surveyed immediately. A shelf is considered full and eligible for a shift when it is three-quarters full, not when books must be piled on the floor. Regular, controlled shifting will prevent sporadic, unplanned shifts, although occasional large-scale shifting cannot be avoided in a growing collection. Whether the shift is major or minor, the move should be structured to eliminate intermediate shifting. Unnecessary shifting increases wear and tear on library materials. William Jesse's pamphlet, *Shelf Work*, is an excellent manual on shelving and housekeeping, and should be kept in every library.

Physical Processing

Preservation and maintenance begin when a new book first comes into the library, not when the book starts to show wear. The acquisitions staff inspects new books for shipping damage, reversed (upside down) binding, and torn, misprinted, blank, or out-of-sequence pages so that imperfect or damaged books can be immediately returned and exchanged *before* the book has been processed. The cataloging staff can aid preservation of newly acquired books by making sure that titles are not underscored, call numbers are not written in the book, color plates and fore edges are not stamped, and other harmful practices are not followed.

Each new book should be handled with great care because the new book of today may be the rare book of tomorrow. Each library must decide how extensively it must mark its books to protect them from loss or theft. Some markings, such as ownership identification, book pockets, and spine labels are necessary, but they should not irreparably damage the books before they reach the shelves and readers. Only soft lead pencils (never ink) should be used in cataloging, and water-soluble paste (e.g., wheat paste) should be used to attach book pockets and book plates. When end papers have maps or pictures or are marbleized, book plates and pockets can be affixed to the verso of the flyleaves. If an identifying mark must be made on a color plate, a pin hole in some predetermined place will identify ownership. Above all, paper clips, staples, cellophane tape, pens, rubber bands, acid paper, and paste should be banned from the processing area. The entire library staff must be made aware of the ill effects of these tools. Paper clips and staples leave rust marks and perforations; cellophane tape yellows, warps, and cannot be removed without damaging paper and print; ink marks permanently; rubber bands cut paper edges; and acid in paste, book cards, and book pockets migrates to hasten paper deterioration.

Binding

Almost every library regularly budgets funds for binding its materials, particularly serial publications, but too often there is no written binding policy. Each library must decide what, when, and how to bind, considering its objectives and its retention and discard policies. Materials to be bound should be catagorized in terms of function and use, with items considered basic to the collection receiving priority treatment.

Most permanent material in museum libraries is given a standard binding. Unique or valuable material should be fine-bound, that is, hand sewn, de-acidified (if necessary), bound in leather or partial leather with gold spine stamping and perhaps with decorative tooling. Folio-sized volumes, atlases, and newspapers can usually be given standard bindings, but frequently used materials may require heavier binding with sewn tapes. Old and fragile materials that cannot be bound because of brittle paper may require extensive hand repair, but slip cases or Solander boxes* generally are used to protect them. When rare, fragile, costly, or bulky materials must be retained as a permanent part of the collection, microfilming should be considered to satisfy the needs of the general reader. Excellent guidelines for categorizing library materials for binding and for establishing a binding policy can be found in Maurice Tauber's *Library Binding Manual*.

It is important to pick a reputable binder who can offer intelligent advice, but the binder should not make policy decisions. Specifications for binding various types of materials should be part of both the binding policy and the contract with the binder. At present there is extensive discussion as to what constitutes a good library binding. Keeping abreast of current literature and understanding the various methods of binding are helpful in establishing binding specifications for each library collection.

Mending and Restoration

Although maintenance, binding, technical processing, and housing are all important in preserving a collection, every librarian should also have some knowledge of mending and restoration techniques. A primary rule is never to allow an untrained person to mend or restore any books, papers, films, or art objects. Permitting untrained people to treat library materials may cause irreversible damage. It is better simply to wrap the item in acid-free paper. While several excellent manuals are available (see bibliography), sophisticated restoration should not be attempted without prior training and experience. Materials used in restoration must be of archival quality, and even simple repairs should be practiced on a discard before work is begun on a valuable item. With these provisos, it is possible to perform minor repairs safely, make wrappers and boxes, and encapsulate materials in mylar. A good mending manual has yet to be written, but the Library

---

*A book-shaped box for holding prints, books, pamphlets, etc., named for Daniel C. Solander, its inventor.

of Congress's *Preservation Leaflets* and Carolyn Horton's *Cleaning and Preserving Bindings and Related Materials* provide valuable advice and instructions. Visiting restoration studios, attending workshops, and reading available literature will sensitize the museum librarian to the need for a conservative approach to restoration.

If funds are available for professional restoration, the librarian should investigate the qualifications and recommendations of the restorer. The Preservation Office of the Library of Congress and the Preservation of Library Materials Section of the Resources and Technical Services Division of the American Library Association will answer questions on the archival quality of specific preservation products and papers, the safety of specific restoration techniques, disaster recovery, and other preservation problems. However, preliminary investigation of the professional literature is advisable before approaching the Preservation Office or ALA staff. Questions that can be easily answered in the literature should not be forwarded.

Apart from fine hand restoration and binding, many steps can be taken to prevent deterioration, preserve paper and bindings, and extend the life of the most fragile library materials. Even in libraries that cannot afford expensive hand restoration, there may be an exceptional volume for which funds can be found. Librarians should familiarize themselves with the terminology, processes, and problems of preservation and restoration. With a knowledge of restoration, a start can be made to categorize books that need attention. Categories might include: volumes that merit binding by a rare book binder (rare materials, leather-bound books, badly deteriorated items, and books containing numerous colored plates); material requiring cases (brittle paper, parchment bindings, and fine bindings with metal studs that damage adjacent books); books with leather bindings in fair-to-good condition that require touching up, cleaning, and oiling (this can be done by librarians, trained clerks, or volunteers); books to be mended (loose and torn pages, loose or warped binding); material to be wrapped in acid-free paper or envelopes (including brittle pamphlets that cannot be placed in pamphlet binders, and badly damaged books that do not warrant extensive handling); and materials that need cleaning with wallpaper cleaner and soft rubber erasers.

The necessity of using only acid-free papers, glue, and mending tape on library materials cannot be overemphasized because high acidity is the major cause of paper deterioration. Mass deacidification and lamination are not feasible for most libraries because of the expense. When the need to deacidify or to laminate a particularly rare or valuable item arises, a reliable laboratory or conservator must be found. It is not a task for an unskilled staff member.

Many museum library collections include prints, maps, original watercolor paintings, manuscripts, archives, and artifacts that must be protected. Watercolor and oil paintings should be wrapped in acid-free lining paper designed to protect pictures and paintings in storage. Acid-free folders should be used to house prints, maps, and archival materials, with prints and maps placed on folio shelving, and manuscripts and archives in acid-free manuscript boxes. Large sheets must not be folded because they will break, fray, and deteriorate along the fold; inexpensive folders and wrappers made of acid-free materials can be easily made for them in the library.

Conclusion

A neglected library collection without rudimentary preventive maintenance will deteriorate beyond repair, but every museum library can ensure the survival of its collection for future generations of researchers by implementing a written statement of maintenance policies and procedures for bindery preparation, physical processes, mending, shelving, and restoration.

NOTES

1. R. W. Church, ed. "Deterioration of Book Stock: Causes and Remedies," *Virginia State Library Publications* 10 (1959).

BIBLIOGRAPHY

Agrawal, O. P., ed. *Conservation in the Tropics.* Rome: International Centre for Conservation, n.d.
Archer, Richard, ed. *Rare Book Collections: Some Theoretical and Practical Suggestions.* Chicago: American Library Association, 1965.

Baker, John P., "Restoration of Library Materials." *Library Scene* 3 (December 1974):4–6.

Baker, John P., and Soroka, Marguerite C. *Library Conservation: Preservation in Perspective*. New York: Academic Press, 1978.

Banks, Paul N., *Preservation of Library Materials*. Chicago: Newberry Library, 1978.

Bohem, Hilda. *Disaster Prevention and Disaster Preparedness*. Berkeley, Calif.: Library, University of California, 1978.

Clapp, Anne F. *Curatorial Care of Works of Art on Paper*. 3d ed. Oberlin, Ohio: Intermuseum Conservation Association, 1978.

Clarke, Carl D. *Pictures, Their Preservation and Restoration*. Butler, Md.: Standard Arts Press, 1959.

Cockerell, Douglas. *Bookbinding and the care of books*. 5th ed. London: Pitman, 1953.

Cockerell, Sidney. *The Repairing of Books*. London: Sheppard Press, 1958.

The Corning Flood: Museum under Water. Corning, N.Y.: Corning Museum of Glass, 1977.

Cunha, George M. *Conservation of Library Materials*. 2d ed. 2 vols. Metuchen, N.J.: Scarecrow Press, 1972.

Diehl, Edith. *Bookbinding: Its Background and Technique*. 2 vols. New York: Hacker Art Books, 1965.

Doloff, Francis W., and Perkinson, Roy L. *How to Care for Works of Art on Paper*. Boston: Museum of Fine Arts, 1971.

Doms, Keith, issue ed. "Preservation of Library Materials." *Pennsylvania Library Association Bulletin* 28 (November 1973). Entire issue devoted to preservation.

Duckett, Kenneth W. *Modern Manuscripts: A Practical Manual for Their Management, Care and Use*. Nashville, Tenn.: American Association for State and Local History, 1975.

Ellis, Rober. *The Principles of Archive Repair*. London: School of Printing and Graphic Arts, 1951.

Glaister, Geoffrey A. *Glossary of the Book*, 2d ed. Berkeley, Calif. University of California Press, 1979.

Greathouse, Glenn A., and Wessel, Carl J. *Deterioration of Materials: Causes and Preventive Techniques*. New York: Van Nostrand Reinhold, 1954.

Horton, Carolyn. *Cleaning and Preserving Bindings and Related Materials*. 2d ed., rev. Chicago: American Library Association, 1969.

Jesse, William H. *Shelfwork in Libraries*. Chicago: American Library Association, 1952.

Kathpalia, Yash Pal. *Conservation and Restoration of Archive Materials*. Paris: UNESCO, 1973.

Langwell, Harold. *The Conservation of Books and Documents*. London: Pitman, 1957.

Le Gear, Clara E. *Maps, Their Care, Repair, and Preservation in Libraries*. Washington: Library of Congress, 1956.

Lehmann-Haupt, Helmut, *Bookbinding in America*. New York: Bowker, 1967.

Lewis, Ralph H. *Manual for Museums*. Washington: National Park Service, U.S. Department of the Interior, 1976.

Lydenberg, Harry M., and Archer, John. *The Care and Repair of Books.* New York: Bowker, 1960.

Mayer, Ralph. *Artist's Handbook of Materials and Techniques.* 3d ed. New York: Viking Press, 1970.

Metcalf, Keyes D. *Planning Academic and Research Library Buildings.* New York: McGraw-Hill, 1965.

Middleton, Bernard. *The Restoration of Leather Bindings.* Chicago: American Library Association, 1972.

Morris, John. *Managing the Library Fire Risk.* 2d ed. Berkeley, Calif.: Office of Risk Management, University of California, 1979.

Morrison, R. W., ed. *Conservation Administration.* North Andover, Mass.: North East Document Conservation Center, 1975.

Morrow, Carolyn C., and Schoenly, Steven B. *A Conservation Bibliography for Librarians, Archivists, and Administrators.* Troy, N.Y.: Whitston Publishing, 1979.

Myers, Gerald E. *Insurance Manual for Libraries.* Chicago: American Library Association, 1977.

Pickett, A. G., and Lomcee, M. M. *Preservation and Storage of Sound Film and Recordings.* Washington: Library of Congress, 1959.

Plenderleith, Harold J. *The Conservation of Prints, Drawings, and Manuscripts.* London: Museums Association, 1937.

―――. *The Preservation of Leather Bookbindings.* London: British Museum, 1957.

Plenderleith, Harold J., and Werner, A. E. A. *The Conservation of Antiquities and Works of Art: Treatment, Repair, and Restoration.* 2d ed. New York: Oxford University Press, 1971.

Polyester Film Encapsulation. Washington: Preservation Office, Library of Congress, 1980.

Protecting the Library and its Resources. Chicago: American Library Association, 1963.

Speyers-Duran, Peter. *Moving Library Materials.* rev. ed. Chicago: American Library Association, 1965.

Swarzburg, Susan G. *Preserving Library Materials: A Manual.* Metuchen, N.J.: Scarecrow Press, 1980.

Tauber, Maurice. *Library Binding Manual.* Boston: Library Binding Institute, 1972.

Thompson, Godfrey. *Planning and Design of Library Buildings.* 2d ed. New York: Nichols, 1977.

Wardle, D. B. *Document Repair.* London: Society of Archivists, 1971.

Waters, Peter. *Procedures for Salvage of Water Damaged Materials.* 2d ed. Preservation Office, Library of Congress, 1979.

Weinstein, Robert A., and Booth, Larry. *Collection, Use, and Care of Historical Photographs.* Nashville, Tenn.: American Association for State and Local History, 1977.

Williams, John C., ed. *Preservation of Paper and Textiles of Historic and Artistic Value.* Washington, American Chemical Society, 1977.

Winger, Howard W., and Smith, Richard D., eds. *Deterioration and Preservation of Library Materials.* Chicago: University of Chicago Press, 1970.

Abbey Newsletter (bimonthly)
  c/o School of Library Service
  Columbia University
  New York, NY 10027

Conservation Administration News (quarterly)
  c/o Robert H. Patterson
  McFarlin Library
  University of Tulsa
  Tulsa, OK 74104

International Bulletin for Photographic Documentation of the Visual Arts
    (quarterly)
  c/o Nancy Schuller
  Art Department
  University of Texas
  Austin, TX 78712

Museum News (bimonthly)
  American Association of Museums
  1055 Thomas Jefferson Street, NW
  Washington, D.C. 20007

PhotographiConservation (quarterly)
  Graphic Arts Center
  Rochester Institute of Technology
  1 Lomb Memorial Drive
  Rochester, NY 14623

Preservation Leaflets (irregular)
  Preservation Office
  Library of Congress
  Washington, D.C. 20540

Restaurator (quarterly)
  Munksgaard International Publishers, Ltd.
  35 Nörre Sögade, DK-1370
  Copenhagen K
  Denmark

Studies in Conservation (quarterly)

International Institute for the Conservation of Historic and
Artistic Works
6 Buckingham Street
London WC2N 6BA
England

Technology & Conservation (quarterly)

Technology Organization, Inc.
1 Emerson Place
Boston, MA 02114

6 Services in the Museum Library

Enid T. Thompson

Museums have five primary responsibilities: to collect materials in the subject area designated for the museum; to conserve artifacts and documentation; to study the designated subject area in detail; to disseminate knowledge; and to exhibit the artifacts and documents collected. Acceptance of these responsibilities makes a library essential in the museum. The services of a knowledgeable librarian are equally essential, for without a qualified librarian at least two of the museum's responsibilities cannot be met.

In any agency specializing in service—and a museum library must specialize in service—there are three requirements: staff, stock, and space.[1] Of these three, staff is the first requirement. Even if the library staff consists of one person, that staff member must be trained in the discipline of the museum, knowledgeable in the library techniques necessary to provide service, and above all, genuinely interested in the subject field of the museum. Museums with minimal scholarly or professional standards routinely demand two master's degrees from the professional staff in the library: a master's degree in an appropriate subject field, and a master's degree in librarianship. Art museums require personnel with art history degrees; history museums want a master's degree in history, with a doctorate in hand or in progress; degrees in biology or anthropology are prerequisites for natural history museums.

Beyond subject knowledge, the librarian is expected to have skills in reference work so that the real needs of an inquirer can be ascertained even when they are not clearly expressed. In addition, the librarian must have a thorough knowledge of the specialized reference works in the subject field. The insights provided by various reference sources can introduce new trains of thought to a receptive mind, whether a patron's or the librarian's. A skillful librarian provides not just service and material; perspective often is an additional product of reference inquiry. In his *Art Library Manual*, Philip Pacey points out that while library material is valued for itself, realia will not be generally sought in libraries but *through* libraries.[2] This thought-provoking idea extends well beyond ready reference assistance.

Good service requires the museum librarian to be familiar with the collections and staff of related institutions in the surrounding area, and even throughout the nation. Not only does this knowledge assist the librarian in selection of library materials, it is of utmost importance in guiding a researcher to pertinent subject collections in other institutions. Mere cataloging of library material is not sufficient for support of research. An intimate knowledge of documentary resources as well as books and reference materials is essential.

Finally, good service, as has been stressed earlier in this manual, requires a thorough understanding of the goals, organization, and policies of the institution in which the library functions. Policies differ between private and tax-supported university libraries, between private and public museums, and between research and exhibition museums. The reputation of a museum is built by a unified group of officers and curators working toward common goals by means of common policies. Library service policies must always reflect museum policies; one department or division cannot stand alone in a museum.

When the librarian has mastered these requirements, service to the varied users of the library can begin. The principle by which librarians serve the museum staff, particularly the curatorial and education staff, is demonstrated in the statement that the librarian oversees the museum's documentary collections as the curators oversee its artifact collections. Without close and constant cooperation between librarian and curators, the goals and responsibilities of the museum cannot be met. For both the library and the parent institution, choice of acquisitions, hours of service, and activities are determined by the combined efforts of the professional staff.

Cooperation and communication are of such importance within the museum that the head of a large museum library usually operates primarily as a reference and research subject specialist, with cataloging and administrative routines handled by assistants. Ordinary service routines—the tasks of circulation, interlibrary loans, record maintenance, checking wait and want lists, photocopying, and statistical work—are secondary to reference and research responsibilities. Operational procedures for routine tasks are carried out by clerical staff; the intellectual illumination which occurs in research results from cooperation between the curator and the subject specialist librarian.

Curatorial questions, like most library queries, are of two types: research questions and those which are usually called "ready reference." Research questions, which can encompass the scope and shape of exhibitions, exhibits, publications, and the authentication of artifacts, may utilize the total capacity of the entire museum staff and the complete collection of the museum, both artifacts and documents. Time and practice may be required to develop a partnership attitude with curators who tend to regard librarians as servants rather than as fellow research professionals. The museum librarian should not be a passive part of research activity, the fundamental process for which the library exists.

It must be stressed that the librarian does not by nature and training do only searching and fetching, and none of the analysis. The librarian brings an understanding of search methodology, the value of documentation, and a broad knowledge of resources to any museum research. The curator brings expertise in artifacts, exhibits, and lectures, but the final quality of any museum project rests largely upon the quality of research involved in the undertaking. Both librarians and curators must be educated to recognize that quality research is the result of partnership.

Queries in museum libraries range from very complex to very simple. Inquirers also range from sophisticated to naive. Good service requires the librarian to assist each patron at the level of need indicated. Interviewing a questioner to elicit exact needs is one of the fine arts of librarianship. Techniques for interviewing can be taught and perceptions in dealing with users can be sharpened, but the essential factor in librarian-patron relations is a determination to give each patron the best possible service at a suitable level, whether the patron is a curator, member, schoolchild, or drop-in representative of the non-museum-going public.

Subject inquiries are the basic type of query in all museum libraries. They are presented in person, by telephone, and by letter. Often they arise from personal visits by a researcher, after a formal exchange of letters and a preliminary evaluation of the library's resources. The quality of research assistance to researchers depends upon two things: knowledge of the library's resources and the extent of the search through which the librarian guides the user. One of the pitfalls for the museum librarian dealing with the general public is the tendency to give the casual inquirer more information than needed when an encyclopedia or ready reference answer would suffice, although an oversupply of information is always preferable to an undersupply.

The tendency to provide service in depth, both in quality and quantity of material and insight, is the result of primarily serving subject experts. A museum attaches special importance to the research undertaken in its library by scholars, whose work enhances the reputation of the library and its staff, and attests to the excellence of the museum and its resources.

A scholar using the museum library has the same needs as the curator—staff assistance, well-cataloged collections, and adequate space. Hard work is involved in serving scholars, who seek out institutions in subject fields in which they are knowledgeable. Work with them is usually rewarded, however, by enrichment of the librarian's subject expertise and increased knowledge of the museum collection. Dealing with a knowledgeable researcher is communication of the highest order; there is an exchange of information in both directions.

Long term or intensive use of a museum library by a scholar involves protocol as well as routines. The researcher usually writes in advance of arrival, presenting plans, background, time schedule, and other research requirements. After the librarian answers this preliminary letter, the researcher arrives for an interview during which research needs are clarified, the librarian explains the rules of the library, and both arrive at a better understanding of the research to be accomplished and methods of attack. If the scholar is using the library for the first time, there should be a review of the regulations governing the use of library materials, copying rights, and the form of acknowledgment to be used if the research is published. Written guidelines and signed releases resulting from this interview are useful to prevent misunderstandings.

Students are served in the same way as scholars and curators, with regard for the level at which they are working. Often students, like many other members of the general public, do not identify with precision their own information needs and cannot express their queries succinctly or clearly. Students have a tendency to approach a subject in terms of a sweeping request, when they actually need a specific ready reference answer. The librarian who is skilled in reference techniques can tactfully help the inquirer to clarify a request and then respond to the actual need. Communication skills and a broad understanding of the subject field are essential in this winnowing process. Often the student who has been helped in this way becomes a lifelong friend of the museum and may go on to become a scholar or museum member.

Children occasionally may use the museum library. Children are regularly brought to the museum on school days. Parents of gifted children often look to the museum library for help with specialized questions. In any case, the librarian has as much responsibility to the child as to the scholar in terms of quality of service, if not of depth. However, the librarian has a right to expect the child to have explored, and perhaps exhausted, the resources of the school library and the public library before seeking the assistance of the museum. The museum librarian should indicate this to the librarian, parent, or teacher who directs children to the museum, but it is vital that the child's interest and curiosity be neither belittled nor stifled.

Museums commonly offer special privileges of research facilities and services to persons who support the museum as members. Members may be allowed special access or study privileges. The librarian may undertake research or bibliographic work for them, often assisting with projects more extensively than is usual for the general public. Members expect these services, as they expect admission to museum lecture series and openings of exhibitions. Since many museums could not exist without the support of their members, the practice of offering privileges to museum members has validity, although it has occasionally evoked the accusation of elitism. When directed toward a museum library, the charge of elitism can quite easily be counteracted by providing the general user with the same expert service that the museum member receives.

Although the typical patron of the museum library is considerate, sometimes even a librarian with extraordinarily good communication and reference skills and a thorough knowledge of the subject field can encounter a problem patron. One library has classified such persons as pests (thoughtless, time-consuming patrons who demonstrate no constructive pursuit of knowledge), pirates (dishonest patrons who steal materials), and vampires (patrons who consider their work to be the only worthwhile undertaking in the library and monopolize staff and resources to the point of restricting service to other library users).[3] The means of dealing with problem patrons are the means used with more congenial patrons – careful selection of materials, clearly written library policies and procedures, fairness, responsiveness, and guidance as the patron works.

Outreach programs are sometimes offered to special groups. A librarian who is familiar with the community and the area served by the museum may carry out the museum's mission as well as encourage support for the library and its work by presenting a speech, slide show, or other educational programs at local meetings. On certain occasions, the library itself can be opened for meetings of groups. Librarians conducting an outreach program must be knowledgeable, enthusiastic, and prepared. (See Chapter 7).

Special services are mandated by law for any handicapped person requesting them in any library which uses public money from taxes, grants, or other sources. This requirement is met not only by constructing wheelchair ramps and other aids to physical access, but by being sensitive about personal assistance that might be welcomed by handicapped patrons in the library.

The museum librarian's service extends well beyond answering reference questions and assisting with research projects. Selection of material for the library is determined by inquiries that indicate gaps in the collection and new research directions. Personal contact with patrons, especially scholars and students, is an excellent way for the librarian to keep abreast of the field and to become aware of unmet collection needs. In collection building, guidance from library users can be as valuable as that obtained from book reviews. Patrons can greatly assist the library in acquisition of source materials. Often the first indication that unique manuscript or photographic collections might be available comes from a patron who has a good relationship with the museum library. Archival, manuscript, photographic, and local collections are sometimes not proffered because the owner does not realize their worth to a museum. A patron, acting as a liaison, can alert both the owner and the librarian to the possibility of placing materials in the library.

A written circulation policy should be prepared for even the smallest library so that a system can be established to keep track of borrowed library material. The policy specifies who may use the library and lists regulations for borrowing. In some libraries there may be three categories of users: those who have reading privileges only, those who have reading and stack entrance privileges, and those who have borrowing privileges as well. Borrowers may range from a few curators restricted to using material in their offices to all members of the general public who wish to take materials home. Most libraries prepare charge slips for borrowed items in duplicate, filing them by both call number and name of borrower. If the library has access to a microcomputer, circulation records may be automated. A permanent register of borrowers that lists full name, address (position or school), telephone number, and date of registration is useful. Museum staff members who are terminating employment should be contacted so that materials charged to them may be retrieved.

Informing users of relevant library material is an important service to the entire museum staff. New materials of importance in the subject areas of the museum should be made available first to interested staff members. When new materials arrive, reviews can be circulated to announce their arrival. A special shelf is usually maintained where museum staff can examine newly arrived materials for a week or two. Items can be reserved for borrowers after the examination period. Current issues of pertinent journals can be routed to interested staff whose names are recorded in the file used to check in periodicals. Regularly updated bibliographies of materials on frequently requested subjects should be available to both staff and general users of the library. A list of new acquisitions received during the preceding month (or quarter or year) can be photocopied and distributed to each curator.

Traditionally the museum librarian undertakes literature searching and bibliography compilation for curators, education staff, and the publications program of the museum. Although these activities form the basis of the library's reputation among museum staff, the librarian should consider preparation of bibliographies on the subjects most often requested by the general public. Bibliographies, prepared inexpensively in mimeographed or offset form, are a service to library users and to colleagues in school and public libraries. If there is a strong demand, publication should be considered, as well as the further step of abstracting pertinent articles. Professional colleagues in the museum and in other libraries are especially grateful for abstract preparation.

Indexing of the museum's publications, whether for use by researchers in the library or for publication, is an appreciated library service.

The librarian and the library staff know from experience how users approach research projects. Informed indexing assures that reference information is up-to-date. Indexing of manuscripts, archival material, and other unpublished resources is also valuable. Special training in preparing indexes and guides to manuscript collections is an asset for museum librarians. Work with manuscripts or archival collections should not be attempted without training; untrained but enthusiastic handling often damages the material. Although initially time-consuming, in-house indexing and documentation, whether by hand or machine, greatly increases the depth and efficiency of library research and extends the librarian's knowledge of both the collection and the subject field.

Photocopying, a timesaver for researchers and librarians, has increased the possibility of service to the library patron, but it has presented new concerns. Except in the case of published copyrighted materials (where the Copyright Act of 1976 is explicit), unsupervised, unauthorized, and uncredited copying may cause problems. To minimize difficulties and assure smooth operation of photocopying and photographic services, appropriate forms should be developed to keep track of the material to be reproduced and the number of copies ordered. The forms should indicate the museum regulations dealing with copyright, usage, credit lines, and financial charges. If the regulations cannot be accepted by the patron, the order for copying is not processed. A signed agreement form is evidence that both librarian and patron have understood their rights and responsibilities. Spelling out the patron's instructions in detail on the form assists the photocopying or photographic staff in its work and provides a usage record for the museum. The source of the document of photograph must be clearly noted to assure that it can be cited correctly. Thoroughly filled out forms constitute a permanent property and usage record.

Another area of service involving forms is the interlibrary loan. Interlibrary loan policies should be understood by every library patron. Fortunately, through the use of standardized forms, interlibrary loan procedures have been coordinated throughout the United States and Canada, with only local details to be formulated within each library. In general, a library that does not lend materials to other libraries through interlibrary loans should not expect to request and receive interlibrary loans from others. This is especially pertinent in a library that allows curators to remove material from its collection for long periods of time.

Often when a question cannot be answered, an artifact identified, or a picture or photograph located, the professional relationships established between librarians of similar institutions through membership in such groups as the American Association of Museums, Art Libraries Society of North America, American Association for State and Local History, and Special Libraries Association are of great benefit. If the item must be researched in primary sources, a sound professional friendship with other librarians and curators is invaluable. Time and effort are saved by knowing which institution has the desired material, what its loan policies are, and whom to approach to secure it.

Knowledge of other institutions often ensures the librarian's presence at museum planning sessions. Effective long-term planning requires knowledge of library resources, and the availability of bibliographies of books, documents, photographs, and other potentially useful library materials is a valuable service to the entire institution.

Conclusion

During the quarter-century following World War II, museum libraries expanded rapidly in a period of affluence and rising expectations, but in the last several years museum library services have grown less rapidly. The major difficulty is financial; demand for increased library service remains strong, but resources have often not kept pace. Museum libraries are vulnerable to severe reductions in funding and personnel because their users are relatively few in number. When financial curtailment comes, oftentimes service to users is an immediate casualty because libraries are reluctant to decrease acquisitions for the collection. Ironically, with reductions in staff, hours of service, and protection of materials, service demands on the librarian actually increase. Any reduction in the quality of service endangers the balance of the five functions of the museum: collection, conservation, study, dissemination of knowledge, and exhibition.

An outstanding example of museum librarianship is seen in the Pompidou Centre for Art and Culture which has become a center of

cultural life in Paris. The *library* of the museum—not the museum—
has reported twenty thousand visitors a day, some of whom have
never been in a library before.[4] This is a far larger public than the
museum library world had ever dreamed of serving and providing service on this scale is a challenge. If museum libraries are to survive and
thrive as active service centers, they must adopt both the traditional
police slogan, "to serve and to protect," and the belief that "argument—about science, art technology, and history—must remain a
museum function."[5]

NOTES

---

1. Peter F. Broxis, *Organizing the Arts* (Hamden, Conn.: Archon,
1968), 13–14.
2. Philip Pacey, *Art Library Manual* (London: Bowker, 1977), 389.
3. C. L. Sonnichen, "Dracula in the Stacks," *Wilson Library Bulletin*
51 (January 1977): 419–23.
4. Mimi Dammen, "The Pompidou Centre in Paris," *Bok og Bibliotek*
45, no. 6 (1978):306–7.
5. Neil Harris, "A Historical Perspective on Museum Advocacy,"
Museum News 59 (November–December 1980): 86.

BIBLIOGRAPHY

Adams, Thomas Ritchie. *The Civic Value of Museums.* New York: American
 Association for Adult Education, 1937.
Alexander, Edward Porter. *Museums in Motion.* Nashville, Tenn.: American
 Association for State and Local History, 1978.
Bierbaum, Esther G. "The Museum Library Revisited." *Special Libraries* 75
 (April 1984):102–13.
Brandemarte, Cindy. "Growing Number of Museums Offer Varied Services
 to Public." *Texas Libraries* 40 (Winter 1978):182–88.
Broxis, Peter F. *Organizing the Arts.* Hamden, Conn.: Archon, 1968.
Chapman, John. *Local Studies in Metropolitan Areas.* London: Library
 Association, 1978.
Chase, Judith Wragg. *Reinforcement of a Black Cultural Museum through the
 Development of its Library Resources in the Field of Black Studies. . . .*
 Interim Report. Project No. L0008JA. Grant No. OEG-0-74-7309.
 Supported by U.S. Department of Health, Education and Welfare.

Office of Education. Office of Libraries and Learning Resources. Washington: Government Printing Office, 1976.

Collins, Marie R., and Anderson Linda M. *Libraries for Small Museums*. 3d ed. Columbia, Mo.: Museum of Anthropology, University of Missouri-Columbia, 1977.

Dolgih, F. I. "The Importance of Archives for Science and Technology." *UNESCO Bulletin for Libraries* 29 (November 1975):331-35.

Finley, Ian. *Priceless Heritage: The Future of Museums*. London: Faber and Faber, 1977.

French, Sonia. "Marketing the Art Library." *Art Libraries Journal* 2 (Summer 1977):11-19.

Gothberg, Helen M. *User Satisfaction with a Librarian's Immediate and Non-immediate Verbal-Non-verbal Communications*. Ph.D. diss., University of Denver, 1974.

Harris, Neil. "A Historical Perspective on Museum Advocacy." *Museum News* 59 (November-December 1980):60-86.

Hieber, Caroline E. *Analysis of Questions and Answers in Libraries*. Master's thesis, Lehigh University, 1966.

Houghton, Beth. "Whatever Happened to Tutor Librarianship?" *Art Libraries Journal* 1 (Winter 1976):4-19.

Hull, David, and Fearnley, Henry D. "The Museum Library in the United States: A Sample." *Special Libraries* 67 (July 1976):289-98.

Keller, William. "Special Collections: The Museum Setting." *Wilson Library Bulletin* 58 (October 1983):111-14.

Kimche, Lee. "American Museums: The Vital Statistics." *Museum News* 59 (October 1980):34-40.

The Library and the Research Worker. London: Library Association, 1961.

Lipton, Barbara. "The Small Museum Library." *Special Libraries* 65 (January 1974):1-3.

Malley, Ian. "Educating the Special Library User." *ASLIB Proceedings* 30 (October-November 1978):365-72.

_____. "Research into Practice in User Education." *Art Libraries Journal* 3 (Autumn 1978):17-26.

Newsom, Barbara Y., and Silver, Adele Z., eds. *The Art Museum as Educator*. Berkeley, Calif.: University of California Press, 1978.

Pacey, Philip. *Art Library Manual*. London: Bowker, 1977.

Rosenthal, Robert. "The User and the Used." *Drexel Library Quarterly* 11 (January 1975):97-105.

Saffady, William. "Reference Service to Researchers in Archives." *RQ* 14 (Winter 1974):139-45.

Sommer, Frank H. "A Large Museum Library." *Special Libraries* 65 (March 1974):99-103.

Thompson, Enid. "Commentary on Archival Management and Special Libraries." *Special Libraries* 69 (December 1978):491-92.

_____. *Local History Collections*. Nashville, Tenn.: American Association for State and Local History, 1978.

U.S. Congress. House. Committee on Post Office and Civil Service. Subcommittee on Census and Statistics. *Report on Adequacy and Management of Services Furnished to Scholars and Researchers by Presidential Libraries.* H. Rept. 92–898, 92d Cong., 2d Sess., 1972. Serial Set 12916–1A.

Waldruff, Lynn Ann. *Art Museum Libraries: Functions and Priorities.* Master's thesis, University of North Carolina at Chapel Hill, 1977.

7 The Role of the Museum Library in Support of Educational and Outreach Programs

Minda A. Bojin and Leslie H. Tepper

A key element in the definition of any museum is its educational function.[1] Museums collect, preserve, and research the objects in their care, sharing the knowledge gained with scholars and the general public. Exhibits serve as the primary medium of communication and education, supplemented by publication of catalogs and scholarly papers, enhanced by in-house and outreach public programming. The role of the museum library in this educational process is to support and augment the museum as an informal learning environment. Library collections and services are designed to meet information needs of museum staff, but they also serve scholars, amateur researchers, and the museum's general public as well. The museum library is a hybrid of a public, research, and special library, catering to audiences with very different levels of information needs. This chapter examines the ways in which museums and museum libraries endeavor to meet the learning needs of their audiences, and how museum libraries are used to fulfill the educational goals of their parent institutions.

Museums offer a unique educational experience, that of exposure to ideas and to perspectives through observation of objects.

> Unlike all others the museum depends on "real things" as the media of communication. . . . The museum as a communication system then depends on the non-verbal language of objects and observable phenomena.[2]

Museums teach through the experience of seeing, touching, and understanding the object in relation to its original context. Although three-dimensional in space, artifacts are multi-dimensional in teaching capability. Isolated, an object offers a sensory and aesthetic experience; placed in a relationship with other objects, it provides historical, social and/or scientific information.

The educational role of a museum is to increase the visitors' knowledge of a subject and expand their ability to understand and relate to objects and to the museum as an institution. Museum goers learn to become critically aware of an object and to form their own judgments as to its importance, beauty, or craftsmanship. Eventually, by drawing on their own knowledge and experience, regular visitors develop a context in which to understand or "read" an object. Stapp defines this as museum literacy. In her definition, literacy "connote[s] competence in using a complex system of information storage and retrieval," and competence comprises "mastery of the language appropriate to that system as well as familiarity with its institutional environment."[3] Museum literacy is thus the ability to read objects and to understand and use the museum's facilities to the fullest extent.

The museum library supports this educational process through its collections, staff, and service. Since most museum visitors and staff already possess a degree of "library literacy," they are able to use the library's facilities to augment the museum's informal learning experience. The collections of print and audiovisual materials serve the museum staff in the research and preparation of programs and assist general visitors to develop a broader context for understanding the museum exhibits. The library staff, who should think of themselves as educational facilitators, supplement the learning activities in the galleries. Librarians assist would-be learners to focus their learning experience, articulate their needs, and identify the kinds of information they require. As Dorothy Mackeracher notes, librarians

> have a unique opportunity to influence learning activities by providing the material resources and human services to assist learners as they extract information and ideas through reading, hearing or seeing the meaning and values which others have given to live experiences.[4]

Within the context of museum education, the library meets the learning requirements of two separate groups. It is a resource for museum professionals concerned with museum education and the ways visitors learn from objects. It provides the visitor with an opportunity to continue the learning process beyond the gallery experience. To identify the needs of both groups, the museum librarian must maintain relationships "that are based not on dependency and authority, but on mutual respect and collaborative attitudes and skills."[5]

Support for the Exhibit Staff

Ideally the curator, designer, and educator collaborate in the production of museum exhibits; each specialist contributes a unique expertise. The librarian also works as a member of this team, supporting each stage of exhibit design and development.

The curator ensures that the object is accurately presented within its framework, story line, or thematic concept. This requires research in the library's collection of books and other materials in order to document the objects and to understand the environment from which they come. The librarian assists by providing comprehensive bibliographies or surveys of the literature. The librarian helps the curator to gain access to additional information sources, including other libraries, archives, professional associations, individuals, and machine readable sources.

The designer, in determining the visual impact of the object and the aesthetic flow of the exhibit, requires three kinds of information from the library. Material of a general nature may be necessary to familiarize the designer with the exhibit topic. Information within the designer's own field of expertise, such as design theory, layout, and technologies for printing processes is required. Finally, literature on museum display techniques is needed to assist in the choice of equipment, lighting, labelling, security system, and proper procedures for artifact preservation. The librarian monitors sources of information on all of these topics and keeps the designer aware of new developments.

Following pedagogical principles, the museum educator tries to ensure that the object communicates its information. The librarian assists the education staff by supplying information about resources and publications in the field of education and museum interpretation.

The librarian can also make an independent contribution to the planning and preparation of an exhibit. Books, drawings, maps, sound recordings, newspapers, and photographs from the library collection are often appropriate for inclusion in an exhibit. Having been trained to identify and acquire archival and manuscript materials, the librarian can provide information on their provenance, use, and history. The correct copyright and crediting procedures may also be the librarian's responsibility.

The museum library plays a vital role in the continuing education and training of museum personnel. Although opportunities for museological study at colleges and universities have improved recently, on-the-job training remains the norm, and materials on museum theory, philosophy, history, and technology should be acquired by the library. By providing the appropriate resources the museum library becomes a center for staff training and development. The process of continuing education is facilitated by the availability of traditional library services: timely delivery of information and documents; routing of journals, articles, and tables of contents of interest to users; regular compilation of bibliographies in specific fields; analysis of the collection to assess its responsiveness; and regular formal or informal consultation with museum staff to determine current and future information needs.

After the opening of an exhibit, the librarian's educational function continues, but attention is shifted from the needs of the museum staff to those of the visitor. This new clientele places additional demands on the collection and requires a different focus for the services of the library. The librarian now becomes a working member of a team of educators and public relations staff concerned with museum education through public programing.

Services for Museum Visitors

Museum visitors, who are the potential users of the museum library, can be differentiated by age, knowledge, and demand made upon the museum's programs. S. Dillon Ripley, secretary of the Smithsonian Institution, identified three audiences who use the museum as an educational resource.[6] Children up to high school age should find museums to be places of fun and exploration with opportunities for both indirect and formal learning. Adult visitors participate in directed teaching experiences, such as lectures, tours, seminars, and workshops. Curators, professors, and amateur researchers interested in advanced study comprise the final group. To Ripley's audiences can be added a fourth: families and tourists who come to the museum not for a formal learning experience, but for the "educational exposure" to ideas through objects.

The library materials available to the museum visitor are the same materials that are acquired to meet the disparate needs of the museum staff. Books and archives used by the curators answer the questions of the professional and amateur researcher, while the less specialized background information gathered for the designer serves the general audience. Museum educators order materials for the use of school and even preschool children as part of their teaching programs. The librarian must analyze the visitors' requests in order to direct them to materials at the appropriate learning level.

The librarian provides the visitor with the traditional library services and also on occasion prepares special programs. The librarian answers reference questions and/or directs the visitor to the appropriate curator for assistance, provides access to the library collection, and suggests additional readings. In addition, attractively printed bibliographies on various exhibit topics are often compiled for visitors and the most relevant books and articles displayed for easy reference or browsing. The librarian may also set up a special exhibit in the library to complement the exhibits in the galleries. Books, drawings, photographs, and sometimes even three-dimensional objects from the library collection can explore a theme related to the gallery exhibits.[7] Finally, the librarian may prepare an article or annotated bibliography as a contribution to an exhibit catalog or other publication.[8]

Some museums have combined a resource center with traditional library services to serve a wide variety of museum audiences. The resource center offers flexibility of collection use and services, and provides a wide range of materials to meet all levels of need. The Royal Ontario Museum in Toronto has established a resource center to serve general visitors, with a special emphasis on school groups.[9] The Boston Children's Museum has also developed a large resource center that utilizes various media, including recordings, curriculum units, slides, and tapes to help the visitor investigate eight defined subject or "study areas."[10]

Although exhibits and associated gallery activities are the major medium of visitor education, museums with additional resources of staff, money, and time often develop outreach programs as a means of extending the museum experience. Attention is usually directed to schools, but may also be extended to institutions such as nursing homes, prisons, or hospitals. Outreach programs increase awareness of the museum's presence and attract new audiences. Museums send packages of information (usually printed materials or slide-tape presentations) to schools to familiarize the students with the building and exhibits before a museum visit; teachers receive suggestions for follow-up activities and lists of books for further reading. In programs for audiences in institutions, museum educators often circulate artifacts as a "hands on" activity to illustrate a lecture or workshop and may also distribute lists of suggested readings to interested members of the audience. For people who cannot or do not come to the museum, artifacts, replicas, and/or specimens are regularly packaged in "loan boxes," "trip-out trunks," or "edu-kits." These are almost always accompanied by print and audiovisual materials, with suggestions for further activities and reading.

The librarian can and should work with the educator in the design and development of outreach programming. A profile of the local community in terms of age, sex, income, education level, and population distribution should be established. The librarian can then recommend audiovisual and print materials suitable for lectures or inclusion in multimedia kits, as well as follow-up readings and references.

The trained librarian can offer valuable expertise and professional perspective on the establishment of public educational programming. The literature of librarianship extensively covers the theory and practice of outreach programming and bibliotherapy. Libraries have developed and tested multimedia kits and visiting activities for the elderly, shut-in, handicapped, preschool, and other audiences with special needs. Skills and experiences from the library world are relevant to programming in museum education and should be shared by the librarian with colleagues on the museum staff.

The museum librarian is a member of a network of professionals that links the museum with other educational and public service institutions in the community. By maintaining working relationships with the staff and patrons of local community, school, and college libraries, the librarian can disseminate information about the museum's resources, roles, and activities. These relationships are valuable in establishing new educational resources and opportunities for the museum educator.

Conclusion

The museum library plays a central role in helping its parent institution perform its educational function by providing the extensive collection and searching services of a research library, the current materials and awareness programs of a special library, and the general collections and public education activities of a community library. The museum must be able to serve the educational needs of audiences ranging from professionals seeking the technical literature of museology and specialized subject fields to school children on a museum visit. As a professional with expertise and knowledge in library science, the librarian can contribute a great deal to the growth and development of the museum's public programming policy and activities.

The potential of the educational role of the library within the larger institution is often not recognized by museum administrators and other members of the museum staff. The expertise in the field of public education and communication which the librarian has gained through training and experience is often ignored to the detriment of the museum as a whole. In a recent study, the author concluded that librarians must work harder to make museums aware of their potential contribution.

> The message for librarianship is that museums are a mission field. For the practitioner, there are opportunities for professional involvement and vital service projects, particularly in bringing a collection from an informal state to one commanding the respect of the museum staff. For library educators, there is the challenge of preparing professionals who

understand museum philosophy, know museum methods and are able to work with museum administrators and staff in developing facilities and collections which will support the mission of the museum and enrich the lives of the people in the community it serves.[11]

NOTES

1. G. Ellis Burcaw, *Introduction to Museum Work*. 2d ed., rev. and exp. (Nashville, Tenn.: American Association for State and Local History, 1983), 13–14. Burcaw offers several definitions of museums from a variety of sources, all of which emphasize the museum's role as an educational institution.
2. Duncan F. Cameron, "A Viewpoint: The Museum as a Communications System and Implications for Museum Education," *Curator* 11 (March 1968):34.
3. Carol B. Stapp, "Defining Museum Literacy," *Roundtable Reports: Journal of Museum Education* 9 (Winter 1984):3.
4. Dorothy Mackeracher, "The Librarian and the Learner: There's More to Learning than Meets the Eye," *Library Trends* 31 (Spring 1983):599.
5. J. Roby Kidd, "Learning and Libraries: Competencies for Full Participation," *Library Trends* 31 (Spring 1983):540.
6. S. Dillon Ripley, "Museum and Education," *Curator* 11 (September 1968):183–87.
7. Nina J. Root, "Biography of a Museum Library," *Curator* 26 (September 1983):185–98.
8. Barbara Lipton, "The Small Musuem Library," *Special Libraries* 65 (January 1974):1–3. Note the range of suggested programs.
9. Rosemary Murray, "R.O.M.: Toronto's Royal Ontario Museum and Its Libraries," *MAHD Bulletin* 4 (Fall 1973):6.
10. Caryl-Ann Feldman, "Museum Library Services," in *The Role of a Library in a Museum*, Valerie Monkhouse and Rhoda S. Ratner, eds. (Boston: American Association of Museums/Canadian Museums Association, 1980), 10.
11. Esther G. Bierbaum, "The Museum Library Revisited," *Special Libraries* 75 (April 1984):113.

America's Museum: The Belmont Report; A Report to the Federal Council on the Arts and Humanities by a Special Committee of the American Association of Museums. Washington, D.C.: American Association of Museums, 1969.

Bierbaum, Esther G. "The Museum Library Revisited." *Special Libraries* 75 (April 1984):102–13.

Burcaw, G. Ellis. *Introduction to Museum Work.* 2d ed., rev. and exp. Nashville, Tenn.: American Association for State and Local History, 1983.

Cameron, Duncan F. "A Viewpoint: The Museum as a Communications System and Implications for Museum Education." *Curator* 11 (Spring 1968):33–40.

Kidd, J. Roby. "Learning and Libraries: Competencies for Full Participation." *Library Trends* 31 (Spring 1983):525–42.

Knox, Alan B. "Counseling and Information Needs of Adult Learners." *Library Trends* 31 (Spring 1983):555–68.

Lipton, Barbara. "The Small Museum Library." *Special Libraries* 65 (January 1974):1–3.

Mackeracher, Dorothy. "The Learner and the Library: There's More to Learning than Meets the Eye." *Library Trends* 31 (Spring 1983):599–618.

Monkhouse, Valerie, and Ratner, Rhoda S., eds. *The Role of a Library in a Museum.* Boston: American Association of Museums / Canadian Museums Association, 1980.

Murray, Rosemary. "R.O.M.: Toronto's Royal Ontario Museum and Its Libraries." *MAHD Bulletin* 4 (Fall 1973):6–7.

Ripley, S. Dillon. "Museums and Education." *Curator* 11 (September 1968): 183–87.

Root, Nina J. "Biography of a Museum Library." *Curator* 26 (September 1983):185–98.

Stapp, Carol B. "Defining Museum Literacy." *Roundtable Reports: Journal of Museum Education* 9 (Winter 1984):3–4.

Stowie, Stephanie H. "Museum Libraries and the Educational Process." *MAHD Bulletin* 7 (Fall 1976):12–15.

Strable, Edward G., ed. "Special Libraries: A Guide for Management. New York: Special Libraries Association, 1966.

8 Basic Reference Tools and Professional Resources

Julie Diepenbrock Herrick

Before users can be adequately served, the museum library collection must include three types of information resources: materials to support research in the subject area of the museum, works on museum administration, and library science tools for the library staff.

Although major reference works in the fields of art, history, and science are discussed in most accredited library schools, students are not normally introduced to basic museology works. Because certain tools of the trade should be familiar to all museum librarians, this chapter will treat specialized tools for the museum reference collection and indicate museology organizations that can be used as resources by the museum librarian. Attention will also be given to library science reference tools and professional library organizations. The suggested readings on museums and museum librarianship will acquaint the librarian with the nature of museum libraries.

Museum Library Operation

The quality of books and journal articles that discuss museum library operation varies widely. Whether written by librarians or other museum professionals, the authors' training and experience must be considered by the museum librarian who is establishing procedures.

A distinction should be made between general publications on the organization and services of the library and those which treat special library problems, such as working with a particular type of material or providing a unique service. The general publications indicate the basic standards established by the library profession, but publications that deal with special problems often fall into the category of "how-we-do-it-good-in-our-shop," and should be used with caution. The librarian must be especially watchful of suggested solutions regarding library administration to be sure that they meet the standards set by the professional library associations.

In general, it is best for the museum librarian to rely on publications of professional librarians and such professional library associations as the American Library Association and the Special Libraries Association. Publications from museum-related organizations or individuals who are not trained professional librarians are likely to be superficial, limited in scope, and misleading. Even the few publications written by trained museum librarians tend to be limited to the initial organizational period of the library or the maintenance of a very small collection and fail to address the administration of a medium-sized or large collection. To date, no single book has covered all phases of museum library work adequately.

The only manual for the museum librarian written with the authorization of a professional library association is the *Art Library Manual* of the Art Libraries Society / United Kingdom. It is a necessity for all art museum librarians. Despite its British orientation, this work is very useful for American art librarians as well. It must be stressed, however, that although the book presents a very full treatment of art library management, it is not a substitute for professional training in librarianship. The following titles will be helpful to the museum librarian when supplemented by professional knowledge and the advice of a professional librarian.

Libraries for Small Museums by Marcia R. Collins and Linda Anderson could serve as a case study of the development of a library in a small anthropology museum with limited resources. Written by museum librarians for persons without professional library training, it is correct in principle, although too brief and elementary for the professionally trained librarian. Nevertheless, it is valuable for its remarks on assessing the need for a library and establishing a collection policy based upon the interests of the museum staff.

Natural history museums are treated by Sydney Anderson in "It Costs More to Store a Lion than a Mouse," a March 1973 *Curator* article, which places the library within the broader perspective of the museum. It discusses the interrelationship of the museum library with museum collections in a total system of resources for research, estimating the cost of each element.

Several works dealing with libraries in historical agencies have been published by the American Association for State and Local History (AASLH). *The Library in the Small Historical Society* (Technical Leaflet No. 27) by David Kaser is a concise summary of technical procedures. Intended for the library staff without professional training, it includes lists of suppliers of library materials and a basic bibliography.

A major source of information published by AASLH is *A Bibliography on Historical Organization Practices* by Frederick L. Rath and Merrilyn R. O'Connell, an expansion of their earlier *Guide to Historic Preservation, Historic Agencies, and Museum Practice*. The *Bibliography* provides a list of sources useful to the staff of a small historical museum or historical society. Planned as a six-volume work, five volumes have been issued to date: *Historic Preservation, Conservation of Collections, Interpretation, Documentation,* and *Administration*. The second and fifth volumes, in particular, discuss topics of interest to the librarian of a historical museum. Because the material relating to the museum library is intended for museum staff members without professional library training, the work would have been more helpful if descriptive annotations had been provided for at least the most important entries.

Another useful AASLH publication is Enid Thompson's *Local History Materials: A Guide for Librarians*. This manual, like earlier AASLH works on historical libraries, is intended for the user with no training and little experience in administering historical collections. It covers collecting materials, organizing the collection (books, pamphlets, tape recordings, clippings, drawing, manuscripts, and other types of materials), legal aspects of collection maintenance (including copyright and deed of gift), conservation, processing (cataloging and indexing), services to users, training volunteers, and special projects (including publicity). An appendix lists resource organizations and supply sources, and there is an extensive bibliography. Librarians without knowledge of local history materials will find this book of assistance.

Access to journal literature in the various subject disciplines is achieved through published indexes to periodicals, and the museum librarian should unhesitatingly subscribe to the appropriate indexes in the fields of the museum's concern. The principal periodical indexes are identified and described in Eugene P. Sheehy's *Guide to Reference Books*.

Articles in museum journals are not often cited in commercially available periodical indexes. *Art Index* is the only index that analyzes museology journals (e.g., *Museum* (UNESCO) and *Museums Journal*) and bulletins of individual art museums. Indispensable for library researchers, *Art Index* has increased the number of museology journals indexed, but stops far short of including all important titles. *Museum News* and *Curator* both publish their own annual indexes, and *Curator* has published a cumulative index to its first fifteen volumes.

Extensive indexing of periodicals is performed by the Museum Reference Center of the Smithsonian Institution and the Museum Documentation Centre of the International Council of Museums which index all of the museological journals they receive. Both serve museum professional personnel and provide reference assistance by mail.

Coordinate indexing systems have been used to index museology journal articles and other museum-related materials that are not amenable to conventional cataloging. Donald V. Hague has devised a "classification scheme" specifically for articles in *Curator*, *Museum* (UNESCO), *Museum News*, and the AASLH Technical Leaflets published in *Museum News*. Although Hague suggests that the scheme can be easily expanded to index other museology journals, it encompasses only very broad topics and does not permit inclusion of additional general topics nor representation of narrower aspects of the broad topics presently included. Since natural history museum techniques are emphasized, use of the scheme would be awkward at best in other types of museums. Despite some overlapping of categories, Hague's scheme might be satisfactory in a small natural history library that indexes a limited number of museology-related journals.

The library of the Henry Francis DuPont Winterthur Museum has devised an indexing method for its Joseph Downs manuscript collection which can be applied to manuscript collections in small museum libraries covering a narrow subject field. Used for the Downs collection since the 1950s, the optic-coincidence Termatrex system has been discussed in detail by Elizabeth I. Wood in her *Report on Project History Retrieval* for the Drexel Institute of Technology. The system has been used successfully at the Smithsonian Institution to index books, articles, reprints, and reports on conservation techniques. Because the number of index terms which can be accommodated is limited—a total of 16,000 has been suggested—the usefulness of this system is restricted to a small collection. It could be utilized by a small museum library with a minimum of expense.

If a museum library has access to a computer and a sufficiently large collection to justify computerization, the library can index its own collection by computer. The Conservation Analytical Laboratory Information Center at the Smithsonian Institution has used computer indexing since its collection grew too large for the Termatrex system. Computerized systems for museum collections are discussed in Robert G. Chenhall's *Museum Cataloging in the Computer Age*. If computer system time and the appropriate software are available, computerized indexing is much more complete than Termatrex indexing because it is post-coordinate and many more terms can be used.

Directories

Directories are among the most useful quick-answer tools for museum librarians. A typical question requiring a directory is the request for the address of a staff member in a distant museum, but directories of various kinds are used repeatedly by the librarian for exchanges of museum materials, interlibrary loans, and reference inquiries.

At an absolute minimum, the museum librarian should have the annual *Official Museum Directory* published by the American Association of Museums. For each museum, the directory indicates address, principal staff members, size and type of collections, research facilities (including whether a library exists), and other data. Despite some errors and omissions, this is the most complete listing of museums in the United States.

Because museums that are not members of the American Association of Museums may not be included in the *Official Museum Directory*, other directories are needed. The annual *Directory of Historical Agencies in the United States and Canada* lists historical societies and museums that are members of the American Association for State and Local History. Military museums that are difficult to locate can be found in the U.S. Army Center of Military History *Guide to U.S. Army Museums and Historic Sites.*

Many regional and state museum associations publish directories of museums. Even when no directory is issued, regional associations can often provide information on museums that are not in the *Official Museum Directory.* Names and addresses of regional and state associations are listed in the *Directory* and in the *Guide to Museum-Related Resource Organizations* which will be discussed later.

The Canadian Museums Association *Directory of Canadian Museums* is a counterpart of the *Official Museum Directory.* It is indispensable for any librarian dealing with Canadian museums, although some Canadian museums are included in the American *Directory.* Most Canadian provincial museum associations publish directories of their member museums. Addresses of the provincial associations are found in the *Official Museum Directory,* the *Directory of Canadian Museums,* or the *Guide to Museum-Related Resource Organizations.*

For international information, two directories, *Museums of the World* and *Directory of World Museums,* cover all types of museums. Although neither is comprehensive, *Museums of the World* is larger and more accurate than the *Directory of World Museums.* It contains a list of national and international museum associations with addresses which the *Directory* does not. It is also better for postal addresses because vernacular names and exact addresses are given, although the text is in German. An index by type of collection is provided. In the *Directory of World Museums,* museum names are in English, but with some inaccuracies. The second edition includes many more entries than the first, but omits formerly provided information about collections and museum libraries, the list of museum associations, and the subject index, although it has a bibliography of national museum directories and articles. If *Museums of the World* is not purchased, the first edition of the *Directory* is worth retaining for the list of international museum associations and the index by type of collection.

If funds permit, a third international directory of museums and other educational organizations, *The World of Learning,* is a desirable acquisition, although it includes only the most significant and well-known museums, libraries, and universities in each country.

National directories of museums are available for a number of countries, including Great Britain, France, Finland, Colombia, Japan, Sweden, and the Soviet Union. As an example, museums in Great Britain are listed in the *Museums Yearbook* of the Museums Association, the British counterpart of the American Association of Museums.

Information about national directories can be obtained from the museum association of the country of interest or from the cultural attache in the appropriate embassy in Washington or Ottawa. Current addresses of the national museum associations may be obtained from the *Official Museum Directory*, the *Guide to Museum-Related Resource Organizations*, and *Museums of the World*, or from the International Council of Museums (ICOM) in Paris and the American Association of Museums' International Council of Museums Committee. (See the list of resource organizations at the end of the chapter.) Directories of museums vary greatly in quality, coverage, and currency of information; some are available without charge.

Two basic international directories of specific types of museums are published by ICOM. Natural history museums and science-technology museums are listed in the *Directory of Natural Sciences Museums of the World* and the *Guide-Book of Museums of Science and Technology*, respectively. Although the two directories omit recently established museums, they are helpful. ICOM also publishes directories of collections of specific types of objects, such as musical instruments. Another directory, the *International Directory of Arts*, not only includes museums, but also art galleries, art dealers, collectors, and auction houses. While its coverage is not comprehensive, it is the only reference work that offers international coverage of both museums and other art institutions.

In addition to directories of museums, other directories may have value for the museum librarian. As examples for the art museum librarian, *Who's Who in American Art* provides biographical information about museum directors and museum staff prominent in the art world, and the *American Art Directory* lists faculty of art departments of schools and universities. The *Fine Arts Market Place* is a directory of sources for art supplies and services.

When questions cannot be answered from the museum library reference collection, the librarian must know whom to call upon for assistance. The expensive but indispensable *Encyclopedia of Associations* is a directory of museum-related and cultural organizations, and other nonprofit groups such as trade associations, professional societies, fraternal and patriotic organizations, and hobby groups. For each, the directory indicates address, director, requirements for membership, publications (if any), and other pertinent information.

For regional and special interest museum organizations, the librarian may refer to *A Guide to Museum-Related Resource Organizations*, originally an insert in *Museum News* and now available from the American Association of Museums. It lists organizations that provide services or funding to museums, or sponsor activities of interest to museum professionals. Other museum-related resources are listed in the *Official Products and Services Directory* published by the American Association of Museums. Individuals who are expert in academic, research, or technical fields may be identified in the *Smithsonian Resource Directory* issued by the Smithsonian Institution's Office of Public Affairs. Current telephone directories should be collected as extensively as possible; those for New York City and other large cities are indispensable.

Because of the expense, not every museum library can purchase the latest edition of every directory. Many libraries acquire every second or third edition of less often used directories; for example, a library may purchase each edition of the *Official Museum Directory*, but only every second edition of other directories.

Bibliographies

The museum librarian routinely purchases the subject bibliographies useful to the curatorial staff for research. Bibliographies on individual subjects can be found in Sheehy's *Guide to Reference Books*, library science journals, subject field journals, and publishers' catalogs. Catalogs of the holdings of several major museum libraries are available in published form; an important example is the Metropolitan Museum of Art *Library Catalog*.

Information on the methods and techniques of museum operation is indispensable in a museum library. A general bibliography on various aspects of museum administration in all types of museums is the *Bibliographie Muséologique International*, published for ICOM at the National Gallery of Prague. Although a number of years behind schedule (the latest issue covers 1974), this annual publication is the most comprehensive bibliography on museums, citing books, articles, and technical reports. It is compiled by the ICOM Museum Documentation Center which prepares the brief bibliographies on specific topics of museum administration that appear regularly in *ICOM News*.

Several major museum associations issue bibliographies. The recent Canadian Museums Association *CMA Bibliography* is a list of the holdings of the Association library. Although not the comprehensive bibliography the title implies, it is a useful selection and research tool. Another useful, inexpensive bibliography is G. Stansfield's leaflet, *Sources of Museological Literature*, published by the Museum Association. For historical museum libraries, the previously mentioned AASLH *Bibliography* by Rath and O'Connell offers thorough coverage of museum administration. A final source is the Museum Reference Center at the Smithsonian Institution which has available bibliographies on various museum topics and, upon request, will compile bibliographies on individualized topics; the Center's services are described later.

Works on Museum Administration and Operation

Noncuratorial staff members of a museum often do not think of the library as a source of problem-solving information. The museum librarian can strengthen the library's reputation among the museum staff by building a small reference collection of material on the techniques of museum operation. Two of the most valuable publications are the UNESCO *Organization of Museums: Practical Advice* and the National Park Service *Manual for Museums*. The UNESCO work covers all areas of museum operations and is particularly valuable in a new museum where procedures are being developed; it is also useful in asessing current performance within an established museum. The *Manual for Museums* is a detailed manual of procedures for National Park Service personnel at museums and historical sites. It is especially helpful for the library of a small historical museum or site. A small historical society museum will find Dorothy Weyer Creigh's *Primer for Local Historical Societies* beneficial.

Although more than twenty years old and in need of revision, Carl E. Guthe's *So You Want a Good Museum* remains a definitive text on standards for museums. No longer available in the United States, it can be obtained from the Canadian Museums Association. Museum accreditation is discussed in the American Association of Museums *Professional Standards for Museum Accreditation*, which replaced Marilyn Hicks Fitzgerald's *Museum Accreditation: Professional Standards*, and is now itself about to be revised.

Natural history museum librarians will find Eugene Bergmann's article, "Making Exhibits," in *Curator* invaluable for its suggestions of basic works on exhibit design methods. Some of the suggested titles are equally useful in art or history museum libraries.

Museum Registration Methods by Dorothy H. Dudley is probably the most important manual on museum registration techniques. It remains the most widely accepted authoritative text in this field. Another basic work on registration, *Registration Methods for the Small Museum* by Daniel B. Reibel, deals only with simple manual methods suitable for small history museums. An AASLH publication, Reibel's manual treats the role of the museum registrar and includes sample registration forms and descriptions of techniques. Two important books on registration by Robert G. Chenhall are the previously mentioned *Museum Cataloging in the Computer Age*, which discusses automated systems for registration data storage and retrieval, and *Nomenclature for Classifying Man-Made Objects*, a long awaited vocabulary for physical description of museum objects, suitable for use with either manual or automated systems. Information on the activities of the registrar is provided in *Profile of a Museum Registrar* by Marjorie Hoachlander and "A Survey: Registrars Identify Their Responsibilities" in the first issue of *Registrar's Report*.

Several recent works offer help with other topics related to museum operations. The American Association of Museums has published a valuable book on personnel administration by Ronald L. Miller, *Personnel Policies for Museums: A Handbook for Management*, that deals with the practical aspects of hiring and training staff, affirmative action, performance appraisal and other matters. It would be especially beneficial in a large museum. Record forms are illustrated in the *Museums Form Book* published by the Texas Association of Museums. *Funding Sources and Technical Assistance for Museums and Historical*

Agencies by Hedy Hartman offers museum personnel an introduction to the potentially confusing subject of federal funding sources. Although this type of information quickly becomes outdated, Hartman's data are currently valid, despite some recent changes in the addresses listed. Other sources of information on museum methods are found in the extensive bibliographies mentioned earlier.

Professional Library and Museum Organizations

The annual meetings of professional library associations offer museum librarians the opportunity to discuss topics of common concern. Of the two largest library organizations, the American Library Association (ALA) and the Special Libraries Association (SLA), the Special Libraries Association is more directly concerned with museum librarianship through its Museums, Arts and Humanities Division (MAHD). SLA issues a quarterly journal, *Special Libraries*; a monthly newsletter, *Specialist*; and various general publications. The Museums, Arts and Humanities Division issues a semiannual newsletter, the *MAHD Bulletin*. The association answers inquiries on technical matters, offers consulting services, and sponsors continuing education programs.

Art museum librarians meet professional colleagues through the Art Libraries Society of North America (ARLIS/NA). The ARLIS/NA quarterly, *Art Documentation*, includes features on professional matters and activities; the irregular newsletter, *ARLIS/NA Update*, contains timely newsnotes; and there are occasional technical publications. ARLIS/NA also provides consulting services.

Museum librarians whose collections include archival or manuscript materials usually join the Society of American Archivists (SAA) which issues the *SAA Newsletter*, the *American Archivist* journal, and various technical publications. The organization also answers inquiries, provides assistance on technical matters, and sponsors continuing education programs.

The annual meetings of museum-related organizations offer benefits to museum librarians. The most important museum association for museum librarans is the American Association of Museums (AAM) which maintains standards for museum administration through its accreditation program. In addition to its annual conference, the

AAM sponsors seminars. Its publications include the newsletter, *Aviso*; the journal, *Museum News*; the *Official Museum Directory*; and technical publications. Both library (institutional) and personal memberships are available. At present, librarian members of AAM are attempting to establish liaison with the professional library organizations. AAM members and nonmembers may join one of the six regional AAM conferences, each of which publishes a newsletter and sponsors meetings and continuing education programs. The international counterpart of the AAM, the International Council of Museums (ICOM), publishes a journal, *ICOM News* and excellent technical materials. AAM members who join ICOM through the ICOM Committee of the association receive the committee newsletter.

Museum libraries in Canada should hold membership in the Canadian Museums Association (CMA), which answers inquiries and assists museum libraries in technical matters, funding, and continuing education. The CMA is an excellent source from which to purchase American, Canadian, and UNESCO museology publications. It can often supply out-of-print titles unavailable elsewhere. CMA publications include the quarterly journal, *The Gazette*; the newsletter, *Museogramme*; the *Directory of Canadian Museums*; and technical books. United States museum librarians are advised to join CMA; in recent years Canadian developments in museum techniques have paralleled or anticipated those in the United States. Canadian librarians may also join a provincial museum association, each of which has a newsletter and provides other services.

Conservation information is available in the journal of the American Institute for the Conservation of Historic and Artistic Works (AIC), whose expert staff members provide individualized advice on conservation methods. Other conservation organizations are listed in *Care and Conservation of Collections*, the second volume of the Rath and O'Connell bibliography. Additional information on conservation methods appears in the *Conserv-O-Gram* of the National Park Service of the United States.

There are museum-related organizations of interest to various types of museums. Natural history museum librarians should be aware of the Association of Systematics Collections, which requires no membership fee. Technology museum and science center librarians should know of the Association of Science-Technology Centers (ASTC), which offers institutional membership only. Both organizations answer inquiries from librarians and issue newsletters and other publications regularly.

In addition to ARLIS / NA, several organizations are of interest to art museum librarians. Particularly important are the College Art Association (CAA), which publishes *Art Bulletin* and *Art Journal* and provides placement services; the Associated Councils of the Arts, which publishes a newsletter, directories, and works on technical subjects, answers inquiries, and provides training; and the Association of Art Museum Directors (AAMD) which publishes handbooks on art museum administration.

For libraries in history museums, the most helpful organization is the American Association for State and Local History. AASLH publications include the journal, *History News*; the *Directory of Historical Societies and Agencies in the United States and Canada*; and excellent technical works on museum operation for the small history museum or historical society, which are often suitable for larger history museums. The AASLH provides inquiry and consulting services, and sponsors seminars and other training programs. The National Trust for Historic Preservation provides similar services in the area of preservation.

Several organizations offer bibliographic assistance in museology. The oldest information center, the UNESCO-ICOM Documentation Centre, was established in Paris in 1947. Probably the largest agency of its kind, the center indexes all materials it acquires. Museum professionals and others with a special interest in museology may utilize the information indexed by the center through personal visit or written correspondence. The Documentation Centre also publishes bibliographies on museological subjects. For a complete description of the Documentation Centre collection and services, see the report by Paulette Olcina in the August 1977 issue of *ICOM: A Newsletter of the ICOM Committee of the American Association of Museums*.

An American counterpart of the Documentation Centre is the Museum Reference Center. Established in 1975 within the Office of Museum Programs at the Smithsonian Institution, the Reference Center compiles bibliographies on general museology topics and distributes Smithsonian Institution publications related to museology. Reference service and research facilities are available for museum professionals and interested individuals. Like the UNESCO-ICOM Documentation Centre, the Museum Reference Center acquires all types of museology materials from museums and museum-related associations throughout the world. It has on microfiche all of the monographs and journals in the UNESCO-ICOM Documentation Centre which had been photographed before the copying program was discontinued in 1974. The collections and services of the Museum Reference Center are described by Paula Degan in the February 1980 issue of *History News*. The Office of Museum Programs sponsors workshops for museum professionals, including an annual workshop on museum libraries.

The Institute of Museum Services in Washington, D.C. offers seminars, technical assistance, and a limited inquiry service in addition to providing funding for museum-sponsored projects. The Institute publishes a newsletter, *IMS Update*, and program information.

Several Canadian sources provide reference assistance in museology. Although there is no full-time librarian, the Canadian Museums Association maintains a strong, growing library collection open to museum professionals. The library of the National Museums of Canada has a research collection of museology publications, and provides reference assistance. The library of the Royal Ontario Museum in Toronto also maintains a collection of museology materials.

Sources of Museum Supplies

Locating sources of museum supplies and equipment was difficult until the recent appearance of two publications, one listing United States suppliers and the other, Canadian. United States businesses that supply equipment and services for all types of museums are identified in the annual *Official Products and Services Directory* published by the American Association of Museums. Three alphabetical sections list products, services, and museum-related resource organizations, and there are alphabetical and geographical indexes. In Canada, the Ontario Museums Association and the Toronto Area Archivists Group have jointly published the *Museum and Archival Supplies Handbook*. Intended to supplement the materials used at their seminars, the *Handbook* emphasizes Ontario supply houses but includes suppliers throughout Canada. Information is organized by function and object desired, with a directory of suppliers and an index of objects. Additional sources of supplies are found at the end of this chapter.

An article by Stephanie Stowe in the Fall 1976 *MAHD Newsletter*, "Museum Libraries and the Educational Process," revealed that museum librarians seldom consider themselves to be professional staff members and often are ill-informed about the nature of a museum and the needs of museum staff. The titles that follow are suggested as "required reading" for every museum librarian.

A readable text on museums that explores what staff members do and what activities are undertaken is *Introduction to Museum Work* by G. Ellis Burcaw. Written for graduate museology students, the book provides a thorough introduction to the daily operations of a museum by describing the work of curators, exhibit designers, conservators, and other professionals. After reading this book, the librarian will be at ease in the museum environment and better able to respond to staff needs. A second work that describes the responsibilities of each professional position in a museum is the Canadian Museums Association *Guide to Museum Positions.*

Three comprehensive surveys of the status of museums in the United States are *America's Museums: The Belmont Report; Museums USA: Art, History, Science, and Other Museums;* and *Museums for a New Century.* The first is a "progress report" on museums by the American Association of Museums. The second summarizes a massive survey of museums by the National Center for the Arts, and includes comparative data on budgets, staff, and growth patterns; a concurrent publication by the National Research Center, *Museums USA: A Survey Report,* contains the same information, but supports it with more graphic presentation of the data. The third is a new American Association of Museums survey of trends that will affect the future of museums. Among recent books on present-day museums is Edward P. Alexander's *Museums in Motion.* A standard work that should be in every museum library is *The Museum in America* by Laurence Vail Coleman. The art museum is treated in a work edited by Sherman E. Lee, *On Understanding Art Museums,* a collection of essays by prominent museum administrators on topics of current concern to art museum personnel.

Articles discussing the museum library are scattered throughout professional library and museum journals. Reading them will reward the librarian with ideas for solving library problems and consolation that the problems are not unique. The articles may be found by consulting *Library Literature*, *Art Index*, museology journals, and the bibliographies mentioned earlier, and by contacting museology resource organizations. The bibliography that follows includes both general articles on museum libraries and articles that treat individual technical matters.

Conclusion

There is no dearth of basic reference tools and professional resources to assist the librarian in learning about the museum world and in providing others on the museum professional staff with the means of doing their own jobs better. A deepened understanding by the librarian of the museum's mission should lead to an awareness— which can then be projected and shared with the museum administration and the rest of the professional staff—of the myriad ways in which the library supports, and could further support, the institution's overall objectives and purpose.

BIBLIOGRAPHY

Ahrensfeld, Janet L.; Christianson, Elin B.; and King, David E. *Special Libraries: A Guide for Management*. 2d ed. New York: Special Libraries Association, 1982.

Alexander, Edward Porter. *Museums in Motion*. Nashville, Tenn.: American Association for State and Local History, 1979.

American Art Directory. New York: Bowker, 1898–.

American Association for State and Local History. *Directory of Historical Societies and Agencies in the United States and Canada*. Nashville, Tenn.: American Association for State and Local History, 1944–.

American Association of Museums. *America's Museums: The Belmont Report*. Washington, D.C.: American Association of Museums, 1969.

———. *Museums for a New Century*. Washington, D.C.: American Association of Museums, 1984.

_____. *Official Museum Directory*. Skokie, Ill.: National Register Publishing Company for the American Association of Museums, 1976–. (Continues *Museums Directory of the United States and Canada. 1961–74*.)

_____. *Professional Standards for Museum Accreditation*. Washington, D.C.: American Association of Museums, 1978.

American Library Association. *ALA Rules for Filing Catalog Cards*. 3d ed. Chicago: American Library Association, 1980.

_____. *Anglo-American Cataloguing Rules*. 2d ed. Chicago: American Library Association, 1978.

Anderson, Sydney. "It Costs More to Store a Lion than a Mouse: Libraries, Collections, and the Cost of Knowledge." *Curator* 16 (Spring 1973):30–44.

Art Index: A Cumulative Author and Subject Index to a Selected List of Fine Arts Periodicals and Museums Bulletins. New York: Wilson, 1929–.

Bergmann, Eugene. "Making Exhibits: A Reference File." *Curator* 20 (September 1977):227–37.

Burcaw, G. Ellis. *Introduction to Museum Work*. 2d ed., rev. and exp. Nashville, Tenn.: American Association for State and Local History, 1983.

Canadian Museums Association. *CMA Bibliography*. Ottawa, Ont.: Canadian Museums Association, 1976.

_____. *Directory of Canadian Museums*. Ottawa, Ont.: Canadian Museums Association, 1976–.

_____. *Guide to Museum Positions*. Ottawa, Ont.: Canadian Museums Association, 1981.

Cary, Norman Miller, comp. *Guide to U.S. Army Museums and Historic Sites*. rev. ed. Washington, D.C.: Center of Military History, Department of the Army, 1975.

Chenhall, Robert G. *Museum Cataloging in the Computer Age*. Nashville, Tenn.: American Association for State and Local History, 1975.

_____. *Nomenclature for Museum Cataloging: A System for Classifying Man-Made Objects*. Nashville, Tenn.: American Association for State and Local History, 1978.

Coleman, Laurence Vail. *The Museum in America: A Critical Study*. Washington, D.C.: Museum Publications, 1970.

Collins, Marcia R., and Anderson, Linda M. *Libraries for Small Museums*. 3d ed. Columbia, Mo.: Museum of Anthropology, University of Missouri-Columbia, 1977.

Creigh, Dorothy Weyer. *A Primer for Local Historical Societies*. Nashville, Tenn.: American Association for State and Local History, 1976.

Danilov, Victor J. "Libraries at Science and Technology Museums." *Curator* 20 (June 1977):98–101.

Daughtrey, William H., and Gross, Malvern J. *Museum Accounting Handbook*. Washington, D.C.: American Association of Museums, 1978.

Degan, Paula. "Light Under a Bushel: Smithsonian's Museum Reference Center." *History News* 35 (February 1980):5–8.

Dewey, Melvil. *Dewey Decimal Classification and Relative Index*. 19th ed. 3 vols. Albany, N.Y.: Forest Press, 1979.

Directory of the Natural Sciences Museums of the World. Bucharest: Revista Muzeelor, 1971.

Directory of World Museums. 2d ed. New York: Facts on File, 1981.

Dudley, Dorothy H., *Museum Registration Methods.* 3d ed. Washington, D.C.: American Association of Museums, 1979.

Dunn, Walter S. "Cataloging Ephemera: A Procedure for Small Libraries." *History News* 27 (January 1972):Technical Leaflet 58.

Encyclopedia of Associations. 3 vols. Detroit: Gale Research, 1983.

Fine Arts Market Place. New York: Bowker, 1973–.

"Guide to Museum-Related Resource Organizations." *Museum News* 57 (November–December 1978): supplement following p. 36.

Guthe, Carl E. *So You Want a Good Museum: A Guide to the Management of Small Museums.* 1956. Reprint. Washington, D.C.: American Association of Museums, 1964.

Hague, Donald V., and Hammond, Catherine. "A System for Cataloging Museum Periodicals." *Museum News* 55 (September–October 1977):38–40.

Handbuch der Museen. Munich: Verlag Dokumentation, 1971.

Hartman, Hedy A. *Funding Sources and Technical Assistance for Museums and Historical Agencies: A Guide to Public Programs.* Nashville, Tenn.: American Association for State and Local History, 1979.

Ho, L. C. "Cataloging and Classification of Exhibition Catalogs in the Library of the Metropolitan Museum of Art." *Special Libraries* 66 (August 1975):374–77.

Hoachlander, Marjorie E. *A Profile of a Museum Registrar.* Washington, D.C.: Academy for Educational Development, 1980.

Horton, Carolyn. *Cleaning and Preserving Bindings and Related Materials.* 2d ed., rev. Chicago: American Library Association, 1969.

Hull, David, and Fearnley, Henry D. "The Museum Library in the United States: A Sample." *Special Libraries* 67 (July 1976):289–98.

International Council of Museums. *Bibliographie Muséologique Internationale (International Museological Bibliography).* Prague: Muzeologicky Kabinet pri Narodnim v Praze, 1967–. (Supplement to *ICOM News.*)

———. International Committee on Museums of Science and Technology. *Guide-Book of Museums of Science and Technology.* Prague: International Council of Museums, 1974.

International Directory of Arts. 2 vols. Berlin: Deutsche Zentraldruckerei, 1952/53–.

Irvine, Betty Jo, and Fry, P. Eileen. *Slide Libraries: A Guide for Academic Institutions, Museums and Special Collections.* 2d ed. Littleton, Colo.: Libraries Unlimited, 1979.

Kaser, David. "The Library in the Small Historical Society." *History News* 20 (April 1965): Technical Leaflet 27.

Larsen, John C. "Use of Art Reference Sources in Museum Libraries." *Special Libraries* 62 (November 1971), 481–86.

Lee, Sherman E., ed. *On Understanding Art Museums.* Englewood Cliffs, N.J.: Prentice-Hall, 1975.

Libraries, Museums and Art Galleries Yearbook. London: Clarke, 1897–.

Majewski, Lawrence J. "Every Museum Library Should Have. . . ." *Museum News* 52 (November 1973):27–30.

Metropolitan Museum of Art. *Library Catalog.* 2d ed. 48 vols. Boston: G. K. Hall, 1980. Supplement, 1982.

Miller, Ronald L. *Personnel Policies for Museums: A Handbook for Management.* Washington, D.C.: American Association of Museums, 1980.

Museum and Archival Supplies Handbook. 2d ed. Toronto, Ont.: Ontario Museums Association and Toronto Area Archivists Group, 1979.

Museums of the World (German title: *Museen der Welt*). 3d rev. ed. Munich: K. G. Saur, 1981.

Museums Yearbook. London: Museums Association, 1976–.

National Endowment for the Arts. *Museums USA: A Survey Report.* Washington, D.C: Government Printing Office, 1974.

———. *Museums USA: Art, History, Science, and Other Museums.* Washington, D.C.: Government Printing Office, 1974.

National Park Service. *Manual for Museums.* Washington, D.C.: Government Printing Office, 1976.

Oddon, Yvonne. "Index to the Museum Classification Scheme." Paris: ICOM Documentation Centre, UNESCO, 1971.

Official Museum Products and Services Directory. Washington, D.C.: American Association of Museums and National Register Publishing Company, 1984.

Olcina, Paulette. "UNESCO-ICOM Documentation Centre." *ICOM Newsletter* 4 (August 1977):4.

Pacey, Philip. *Art Library Manual.* London: Bowker, 1977.

Rath, Frederick L., and O'Connell, Merrilyn R., eds. *A Bibliography on Historical Organization Practices.* 5 vols. Nashville, Tenn.: American Association for State and Local History, 1975–80.

———. *Guide to Historic Preservation, Historic Agencies, and Museum Practice: A Selective Bibliography.* Cooperstown, N.Y.: New York State Historical Association, 1970.

Reibel, Daniel B. *Registration Methods for the Small Museum.* Nashville, Tenn.: American Association for State and Local History, 1978.

Sears List of Subject Headings. 12th ed. New York: Wilson, 1982.

Shaw, Renata V. "Picture Organization, Practices and Procedures." *Special Libraries* 63 (October 1972):448–56; (November 1972):502–6.

Sheehy, Eugene P., comp. *Guide to Reference Books.* 9th ed. Chicago: American Library Association, 1976. Supplements: 1980 and 1982.

Smithsonian Institution. *Smithsonian Resource Directory.* 2d ed. Washington, D.C.: Smithsonian Institution, 1979.

Stansfield, G. *Sources of Museological Literature.* 2d ed. London: Museums Association, 1976. (Information Sheet 9).

Stowe, Stephanie H. "Museum Libraries and the Education Process." *MAHD Bulletin* 7 (Fall 1976):12–14. (Published by Museums, Arts and Humanities Division, Special Libraries Association).

"A Survey: Registrars Identify Their Responsibilities." *Registrar's Report* 1 (May 1977):6–7.

Texas Association of Museums. *Museums Forms Book.* Austin, Tex.: Texas Association of Museums, 1980.

Thompson, Enid. *Local History Collections: A Manual for Librarians.* Nashville, Tenn.: American Association for State and Local History, 1978.

Tillotson, Robert G. *Museum Security / La Securité dans les musées.* Paris: International Council of Museums, 1977.

UNESCO-ICOM Museum Documentation Centre. *Museum Classification Scheme.* 3d ed. Paris: UNESCO, 1968.

United Nations Educational, Scientific, and Cultural Organization (UNESCO). *The Organization of Museums: Practical Advice.* Paris: UNESCO, 1968. (Museums and Monuments 9)

U.S. Library of Congress. *Library of Congress Filing Rules.* Washington, D.C.: Library of Congress, 1980.

U.S. Library of Congress. Subject Cataloging Division. *Classification: Classes: A–Z.* Washington, D.C.: Government Printing Office, 1917–.

_____. *Library of Congress Subject Headings.* 9th ed. 2 vols. Washington, D.C.: Library of Congress, 1980. (Annual and quarterly supplements.)

Weihs, Jean Riddle; Lewis, Shirley; and Macdonald, Janet. *Nonbook Materials: The Organization of Integrated Collections.* 2d ed. Ottawa, Ont.: Canadian Library Assocation, 1979.

Who's Who in American Art. New York: Bowker, 1936–.

Wood, Elizabeth Ingerman. *Report on Project History Retrieval; Tests and Demonstrations of an Optic-Coincidence System of Information Retrieval for Historical Materials.* Philadelphia: Drexel Institute of Technology, 1966.

World of Learning. London: Europa, 1952–.

English-language Periodicals of Interest to Museum Professionals

American Archivist (quarterly)
Society of American Archivists
600 South Federal Street, Suite 504
Chicago, IL 60605

Art Gallery (bimonthly)
Hollycroft Press
Ivoryton, CT 06442

Art Documentation (quarterly)
Art Libraries Society of North America
3775 Bear Creek Circle
Tucson, AZ 85749

Arts Reporting Service (biweekly)
8404 Carderock Drive
Bethesda, MD 20817

ASC Newsletter (bimonthly)

Association of Systematics Collections
Museum of Natural History
University of Kansas
Lawrence, KS 66045

ASTC Newsletter (bimonthly)

Association of Science-Technology Centers
1413 K Street, NW
Washington, D.C. 20005

Aviso (monthly)

American Association of Museums
1055 Thomas Jefferson Street, NW
Washington, DC 20007

Conserv-O-Gram (irregular)

Division of Museum Services
National Park Service
Harpers Ferry Center
Harpers Ferry, WV 25425

Curator (quarterly)

American Museum of Natural History
79th Street and Central Park West
New York, NY 10024

Foundation News (bimonthly)

Council on Foundation
1828 L. Street, NW
Washington, DC 20036

Gazette (quarterly)

Canadian Museums Association
280 Metcalfe Street
Ottawa, Ontario K2P 1R7
Canada

History News (monthly)

American Association for State and Local History
708 Berry Road
Nashville, TN 37204

ICOM: A Newsletter of the ICOM Committee of the American Association of Museums (quarterly)

American Association of Museums
1055 Thomas Jefferson Street, NW
Washington, DC 20007

ICOM News (quarterly)

International Council of Museums
Maison de l'Unesco
1 Rue Miollis
F–75732 Paris
France

Journal of the American Institute for Conservation (semiannually)

American Institute for Conservation of Historic and Artistic Works (AIC)
3545 Williamsburg Lane, NW
Washington, DC 20008

Museogramme (monthly)

Canadian Museums Association
280 Metcalfe Street
Ottawa, Ontario K2P 1R7
Canada

Museologist (quarterly)

Northeast Museums Conference
25 Nottingham Court
Buffalo, NY 14216

Museum (quarterly)

UNESCO
7 Place de Fontenoy
F–75700 Paris
France

Museum Magazine (bimonthly)

Museum Magazine Associates
260 Madison Avenue
New York, NY 10016

Museum News (bimonthly)

American Association of Museums
1055 Thomas Jefferson Street, NW
Washington, DC 20007

Museums Bulletin (monthly)

Museums Association
34 Bloomsbury Way
London WC1A 2SF
England

Museums Journal (quarterly)

Museums Association
34 Bloomsbury Way
London WC1A 2SF
England

Roundtable Reports (quarterly)
Museum Education Roundtable
c/o Betty Sharpe
P.O. Box 8561
Rockville, MD 20856

Technology & Conservation (quarterly)
Technology Organization, Inc.
1 Emerson Place
Boston, MA 02114

Washington International Arts Letter (ten issues per year)
Washington International Arts Letter
P.O. Box 9005
Washington, DC 20003

Resource Organizations

American Association for State and Local History
708 Berry Road
Nashville, TN 37204

American Association of Museums
1055 Thomas Jefferson Street, NW
Washington, DC 20007

American Council for the Arts
570 Seventh Avenue
New York, NY 10018

American Institute for Conservation of Historic and Artistic Works (AIC)
3545 Williamsburg Lane, NW
Washington, DC 20008

American Library Association
50 East Huron Street
Chicago, IL 60611

Art Libraries Society of North America
3775 Bear Creek Circle
Tucson, AZ 85749

Association of Science-Technology Centers
1413 K Street, NW
Washington, DC 20005

Association of Systematics Collections
Museum of Natural History
University of Kansas
Lawrence, KS 66045

Canadian Museums Association
Resource Center
280 Metcalfe Street
Ottawa, Ontario K2P 1R7

College Art Association of America
149 Madison Avenue
New York, NY 10016

Institute of Museum Services
330 C Street, NW
Washington, DC 20202

International Council of Museums (ICOM) Committee
American Association of Museums
1055 Thomas Jefferson Street, NW
Washington, DC 20007

Museum Reference Center
Office of Museum Programs
Smithsonian Institution
Washington, DC 20560

National Museums of Canada
2086 Walkley Road
Ottawa, Ontario K1A OM8
Canada

National Trust for Historic Preservation
1785 Massachusetts Avenue, NW
Washington, DC 20036

Society of American Archivists
600 South Federal Street
Chicago, IL 60605

Special Libraries Association
235 Park Avenue South
New York, NY 10003

UNESCO-ICOM Museum Documentation Centre
Maison de l'Unesco
1 Reu Miollis
F–75732 Paris
France

Sources of Information on Supplies

Library Supplies

Bro-Dart, Inc.
1609 Memorial Avenue
Williamsport, PA 17705

Bro-Dart, Inc.
109 Roy Boulevard
Brantford, Ontario
Canada

Demco, Inc.
P.O. Box 1488
Madison, WI 53701

Gaylord Brothers, Inc.
P.O. Box 61
Syracuse, NY 13221

University Products, Inc.
South Canal Street
Holyoke, MA 01040

Archival Supplies

Hollinger Corporation
3810 South Four Mile Run Drive
Arlington, VA 22206

Museum Supplies

The best sources of information are books by the American Association of Museums and the Ontario Museums Association.

Official Products and Services Directory. Washington, D.C.: American Association of Museums and National Register Publishing Company, 1980.

Museum and Archival Supplies Handbook. 2d ed. Toronto, Ont.: Ontario Museums Association and the Toronto Area Archivists Group, 1979.

9 Museum Library Facilities

M. Noël Balke

The facilities of any library comprise the premises in which the library is located; the services supplied to the premises, such as lighting, heat, and air-conditioning; and the furniture and equipment for using and storing the collections. (See Table 1.) In planning facilities for the special library, the policy and philosophy, as well as the budget, of the parent institution are prime considerations since they govern the use of the library, the nature of its collections, and the clientele to be served. Another important consideration is often overlooked, with unfortunate results: only when the librarian is a member of the planning team from the beginning and is regularly consulted can well-informed decisions be reached concerning the location of the library, the structural requirements for the area, and the amount of space needed for the collections, the staff, and the users.

The museum library differs from other special libraries only in the nature of its collections and the variety of its users. In preparing the plans for a new library, the librarian should use his or her experience and professional knowledge to provide the planners with a clear picture of the facilities necessary for efficient library operation.

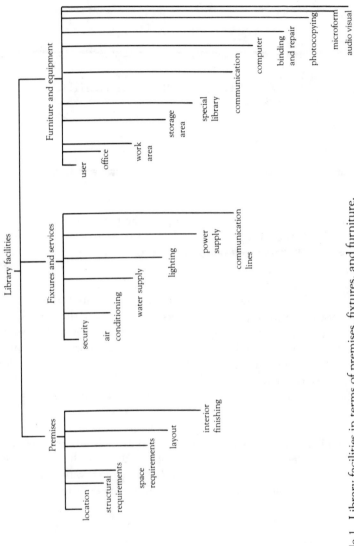

Table 1. Library facilities in terms of premises, fixtures, and furniture.

Location

The convenience of the user is the principal factor in determining the location of the library in a museum. If the library is to serve the public as well as the museum staff, there should be easy access from the public areas of the building, and in order to simplify control by library staff and museum security personnel, there should be only one entrance. A library that is for the use of museum staff only can be located in a nonpublic, office area of the museum; this reduces the security problem. The library stacks or storage areas can be immediately above or below the library reading and office areas, provided there is internal access. Basement storage may be considered if there is no danger of flooding and if books can be elevated sufficiently above the floor. In any case, the library reading and office areas should be located with the requirements, comfort, and convenience of both library staff and all varieties of users in mind.

Structural Requirements

Structural considerations may determine the location of the library within the building and the arrangement of the collections within the library. The strength of library floors should be at least twice that of normal office floors. For efficient use of space, floors should be capable of supporting a load of 150 pounds per square foot as opposed to the 75 pounds per square foot load that is the usual standard for office areas. An engineering study to determine such load factors must be requested for any existing building in which a library is to be located. In planning a new museum building which will house the museum library, the necessary structural requirements can be incorporated in the building plans before construction.

In old buildings the strength of the floor may not be uniform in all areas. Because museums are often located in historic buildings, the museum director who intends to establish or expand a library would be well advised to find the original building plans or consult a building inspector. The convenience of the desired location may have to be subordinated to the safety factor. Rows of library shelving or of filing cabinets may have to be located in the areas with the heaviest load-bearing capability. If movable compact shelving is to be used to help control the future expansion of the library, a minimum floor loading capability of 250 pounds per square foot is required. For greater safety, the weight of the compact shelving and the actual weight per square foot of the material to be stored should be estimated for the engineering study. Microform reader-printer equipment which tends to be very heavy should be located next to load-bearing columns or walls.

<hr>

Space Requirements

<hr>

The actual amount of space required for the library depends upon the size and planned growth rate of the collection, the working space needed by present and future library personnel, and the reading areas provided for users. It must be emphasized here that standard office area allowances are not sufficient for libraries. There are standards for various library areas. Space requirements for reading areas are affected by the decision to use either group tables or individual carrels; for offices, by space needed for necessary shelving and passage of book trucks; for work areas, by such items as computer terminals, catalog cabinets, photocopying equipment, microfilm readers, and sorting tables. Space required for the storage of collections depends upon the nature of the material (bound volumes, documents, microforms, slides, other audiovisual materials) and on the type of storage (stack shelving compact shelving, filing cabinets). The standards quote measurements in square feet for the different library areas and include allowances for aisle spaces and for minimal growth. Space required to allow for the growth expected in the next 20 years can be calculated using the same standards. These standards are to be found in the literature of the library profession, and at this point the contribution of the librarian to the planning process becomes not only invaluable but essential.

It is up to the librarian to ensure that the importance of the library's layout and the interrelationship of the various areas are understood by the planning team. The sequence of spaces within the library must facilitate the flow of materials through the various library processes and provide for the installation of appropriate equipment and furnishings along the way. (See Table 2.) At the same time, the importance of

118

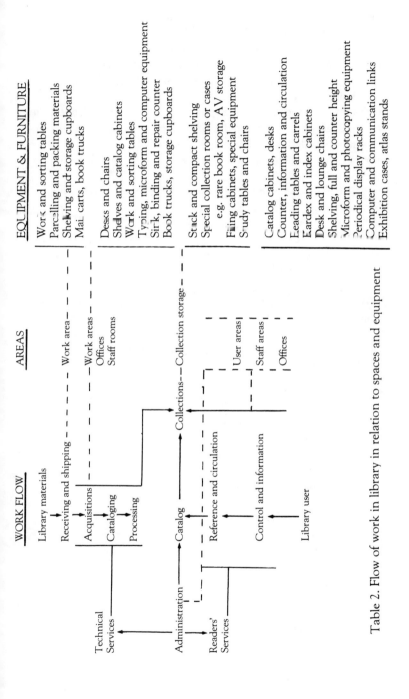

Table 2. Flow of work in library in relation to spaces and equipment

incorporating the principle of flexibility into the design must be emphasized. Permanent divisions between library areas should be avoided except where the need for security makes this desirable, as in the case of a
rare book room. An adjustment in the size of library areas should be possible as changes in staff, collection size, or library technology dictate.

Planning library areas efficiently is as important for small museums
with limited finances, staff, and space, as it is for larger institutions. In
any museum library, a well-designed floor plan is necessary to accom-
modate the collection of library materials; allow for staff work space,
storage, and handling of incoming materials; and provide seating for
library users.

Listed below are the various areas found in a working library.
Established space requirements and specialized furnishings appropriate to each area are indicated.

1. <u>User space</u>. The size of the area for users depends upon the
number of users for whom reading spaces are provided and on the
type of furniture and equipment considered necessary. It is assumed
that only a small percentage of the potential users will be in the library
at one time. The number of these users is fixed when the library serves
only the museum staff. If the library is open to the public, however,
care must be taken when estimating the number of users to provide a
margin of extra seating. In calculating the amount of space needed,
the following figures should be used:

User Space	Square Feet / Person
Individual carrels	30–40
Tables seating 4–6	25
Lounge seating (e.g., for browsing through current periodicals)	30
Closed study areas	40–60
Audiovisual rooms	40–60
Seminar room	25
Microform reading areas	25
Computer terminals	25

Optional user areas which may be incorporated into the
library, depending upon the size and policy of the institution, are a

photocopying unit and washrooms. If the library is not in the same building as the museum, an allocation of space for lockers and coin telephones in the entrance lobby should be considered.

2. <u>Combined user and staff space</u>. In areas open to both users and staff, close attention should be paid to both the flow of people and the flow of library materials. In the public catalog area, the amount of space required will be affected by the type and size of the catalog, which may be conventional card form, book form, microform, a computer printout, or on a computer terminal screen. In each case, the nature of the catalog and the ease of consultation by users and staff determine the size of the area.

In reference or reader service areas and in circulation and control areas, 125 square feet per person should be allowed for clerical personnel and 175 to 180 square feet per person for other library staff. This allocation includes space for a circulation desk, chairs, book trucks, shelving, files, computer terminals, and reference tools. The circulation area may include periodical display racks, signs and bulletin boards, display cases, and, if necessary, some type of security installation.

The library administration should also be accessible to staff and users. Offices for librarians should be between 125 and 300 square feet with adjacent secretarial and clerical areas of between 100 and 125 square feet.

3. <u>Staff space</u>. Although the library user does not normally have access to the technical service areas in a museum library, professional museum personnel may quite often be found there, consulting members of the library staff or searching for material recently acquired but not yet cataloged. A space allowance of 175 to 200 square feet per library staff member should permit movement and housing of library materials during processing.

It is in the technical service areas that planning of spaces to allow orderly flow of library materials is most important. Work and sorting tables, counters, shelves, book and mail trucks, desks and chairs, catalog and index cabinets, and storage units for supplies have to be accommodated, as well as office equipment, including calculators, computer and telex terminals, telephones, typewriters, and binding and repair tools. Staff lounges, washrooms, cloakroom and locker space, and, if the size of the staff warrants, a meeting room may also be included at 15 square feet per person.

4. Collection space. The amount of space to be designated for storage of the library collection can be determined only after taking into consideration the size of the existing collection and its probable future growth, the different types of materials in the collection, and the most suitable storage equipment for each. A small number of rare books may be kept in a secure cabinet; a larger collection will require a rare book room with special fire protection and environmental controls. Large collections of auction catalogs fit very conveniently into compact movable shelving installations. Collections of posters, prints, drawings, and maps need wide horizontal storage cabinets or boxes on wide, deep shelves rather than the vertical shelving that is standard for bound books and periodicals.

Library collections vary from one museum to another, but the common denominator is the bound book on the three-foot-long shelf. All other materials in the collection relate to this denominator, which is used as a basis in calculating the required amounts of storage equipment and space.

Shelving for the general book collection is estimated at an average of seven volumes per linear foot, which allows for some collection growth. This figure is transposed into ten volumes per square foot in calculating the floor space required for a book collection housed on stack shelving. Both figures assume that shelves are two-thirds full. The second figure allows for some collection growth, study tables, and minimum aisle spaces based on four-and-a-half foot shelving centers.

The storage and floor space necessary for nonbook materials can be calculated in terms of bound volumes to facilitate the planning estimates. The space needed for 125 typical books on standard library shelving will also house 45 large reference volumes, 125 computer tapes, 1000 documents (single sheets, small pamphlets, manuscripts, and other archival materials), 400 reels of microfilm in boxes, 10,000 microfiches or microcards in boxes, 7 newspaper titles on display or unbound, 9 bound volumes of the back files of newspapers, 9 current periodical titles on display, unbound current-year issues of 30 periodical titles, 500 phono disc records or tapes, 1000 cassettes, 45 slide carrousels, 125 films and 2250 filmstrips in boxes.

The conversion figures for nonbook material to be housed in vertical files, cabinets, or other specialized forms of storage equipment (again in relation to the 125 volume shelving space) are 105 maps, 315 microfilm reels, 7900 microfiches or microcards, 790 pamphlets, 2560 slides in unbound cases, 5120 slides in bound cases, 580 filmstrips, and 790 mounted photographs.

Fixtures and Finishes

Decorative effect and utility both influence the choice of interior finish for library areas. Large surfaces should be light in color, have a matt finish, and be sound absorbent. Acoustic title on the ceiling and carpeting on the floor will reduce the noise level; acoustic wall panels, fabric-covered movable screens, and curtains or fabric-covered blinds over all glazed surfaces will also be beneficial.

Locating offices and reading spaces in areas with natural light while placing stacks in interior areas will usually obviate the danger of light striking the books, but it may be necessary to shield some windows with venetian blinds or architectural louvers in order to prevent direct sunlight damage to books located on shelves and book trucks.

Floor coverings should be resilient and permit easy movement of both trucks and people. There should be no changes in floor level unless there are elevators or book hoists in the library that permit vertical movement of loaded book trucks.

Both present and future requirements should be considered in arranging for communication lines, telephones, intercom systems, and telex. There should be sufficient electric outlets for equipment such as typewriters, microfilm and microfiche readers, slide viewers, computer terminals, videodisc players, and clocks, with circuits capable of handling the necessary power requirements. In view of the rapidly changing state of library technology, heavy duty lines should be supplied for computer terminals, binding equipment, photocopiers, and other machines that may be required in the future. Water should be provided in the workshop area because of the materials used in binding and repair of books and documents.

Lighting

Lighting needs special attention in a library. The various work, reading, and storage areas require different qualities, types and intensities of light. The level of light must be sufficient for the different tasks to be performed, and the installation should enhance the interior design. Throughout the library the lighting should be diffused, and sources of glare and reflected light eliminated. Fluorescent lighting, where used, should be a warm white, to approximate daylight.

Lighting in offices should be individually controlled, and in the user area different groups of lights should have separate control switches. For most reading and office areas, a light level of 70 foot candles is adequate. For storage areas, 30 foot candles is sufficient, but areas for close work such as map and print inspection, card filing, and book repair, require a 100 foot candle level of illumination. For computer terminals and microform viewers, indirect lighting should be used.

Light of any kind increases the rate of deterioration of library materials, particularly of paper. Fluorescent light contains harmful radiation and all fluorescent fixtures should be provided with screens to filter out the ultraviolet rays. Lighting should be switched off or reduced in areas where no one is working. When a room is subdivided by book stacks, the lighting must usually be increased to provide sufficient illumination to read the bottom shelves. In stack areas it should be possible to switch the lights on and off along each aisle as needed.

Atmospheric Control

In a museum environment it should not be necessary to emphasize the conservation aspect in environment control. It is, however, sometimes necessary to point out to the museum administration that the library collections are a valuable part of the museum holdings and consist of many of the same materials as the museum objects, and that library materials are equally subject to deterioration when housed in unfavorable conditions.

Control of the atmospheric environment in a library is concerned with temperature, humidity, and the cleanliness of the air. The air-conditioning system should operate continuously and be capable of providing filtered air within a preferred humidity range of 45 to 55 percent and an ideal temperature range of 55 to 65 degrees Fahrenheit. Since this is less than comfort level, strict application of these limits will normally be confined to less-used storage areas, restricted stack areas, and rare book rooms. For areas frequented by staff and users, a greater range of tolerance must be permitted—for example, humidity down to 35 percent during the winter in northern climates, and a temperature range of 65 to 72 degrees.

The filter systems supplied with most office air-conditioning systems are usually inadequate. It is to be hoped that the library will be protected by the most effective air filtering system installed for the entire museum building which removes the grit, dust, and gases deleterious to both library and museum materials. If it is not, installation of such a system should be considered, especially in areas that suffer severe air pollution from industrial and other sources.

Air circulation and ventilation control are very important for rare book rooms and special collection storage areas. Areas for book binding and repair, film cleaning, or other special tasks may require exhaust fans to remove fumes and odors.

Security

Protection against fire and theft should be built into the library premises at the time of construction or alteration. Experience has shown that an automatic sprinkler system in which sprinkler heads activated by heat detectors emit a localized water spray is suitable for most library areas. Water is less permanently damaging to library materials than many chemical fire retardants and the water sprayed by a sprinkler head does less damage than water from the high pressure hoses used by fire fighters.

A less destructive means of fire protection may be used for special collections. The additional expense of installing a halon gas sprinkler system may be justified to protect rare book, manuscript, and print rooms, although in most cases the cost would be prohibitive for the whole library.

Locating the library in proximity, horizontal or vertical, to the museum cafeteria, kitchen, or laboratory is to be avoided to reduce the risk of fire spreading to flammable library materials and of damage from water. To further minimize the risk of fire, smoking should be forbidden, or restricted to a controlled area.

The ultimate protection against theft from museum libraries remains the same as against theft from the museum collections: security guards and/or an automatic alarm system. However, as museum security personnel are not usually able to detect the type of library material easily concealed about the person, the public reading areas of the library should be planned to permit easy surveillance by library staff. In the museum library open to the public, it may be worthwhile to consider one of the commercial systems that provides for inserting a device in a book to trigger an alarm if an attempt is made to remove the item from the library in an unorthodox fashion.

Furniture and Equipment

Library furniture for user, office, and storage areas has been indicated in Table 2 and described in the section on space requirements. Most libraries buy necessary shelving, catalog cabinets, carrels, step stools, display racks, and other specialized equipment from established library suppliers. Selection of equipment and approval of furniture acquisitions are the responsibility of the museum librarian.

Sometimes when a new building is being designed, the architect may wish to design furniture and fittings to harmonize with the total concept. Unless the architect is thoroughly familiar with library buildings and layouts, he or she may not be aware that library shelves and periodical display racks are designed on a three-foot module, that there is a standard size for card catalog drawers, and that these require safety rods to hold the cards and safety catches to prevent the drawers from falling out. A few inches one way or the other in the location of a door may eliminate an entire section of shelving. A catalog drawer longer than normal may be too heavy to lift when filled with cards. The importance of having the librarian on the planning team to advise the architect on library standards and specialized equipment and furniture is obvious.

The Small Museum Library

A small museum starting a library or changing its library from volunteer to professional status may appear to present unique problems to those involved. The museum may have a new library and an equally new librarian, or the director may be contemplating inaugurating a library in a building with little space and a minimal budget adequate only for basic facilities. Nevertheless, to make best use of the resources available, the library facilities should be based upon the standards previously outlined. The figures given for calculating user, staff, and collection areas should be utilized to determine the floor space need for the library.

The impetus to start a museum library develops when materials appropriate for a library collection exist in sufficient number within the museum to require organization to make them accessible. The initial step is the calculation of the space needed to house the library materials and any acquisitions to be added in the near future. The next requirement is space for the staff. The budget should be large enough to cover the salaries of a professional librarian, with an assistant for typing and clerical work. In a small library, 175 square feet of office space will be needed for the librarian, 125 square feet for the assistant, and 175 square feet of work area for shipping, receiving, and sorting library materials. If there is any possibility of volunteer or part-time employees, additional working space should be provided so that they do not have to occupy seats intended for readers.

After space requirements for the collection have been calculated, the furnishing of the space is contingent upon the nature of the materials in the library collection. Books, pamphlets, maps, photographs, slides, audio tapes, and other specialized materials all require different housing, and a variety of furniture and equipment is available. The final choice should be governed by the professional advice of the librarian.

Finally, user space remains to be considered. A useful module to use in planning measures 230 square feet. This would include one 6' x 3' group table seating six readers (at 25 square feet per person), and two carrels for museum staff members or research workers who prefer to study alone (at 40 square feet per person). This 230 square foot module constitutes the minimum space allowance for library users; additional modules can be added as needed and as space is made available. Alternatively, the additional space for a module might be used for a periodical browsing area. A low table and lounge seating for two or three persons (at 30 square feet per person) could be placed adjacent to tilt-and-store shelving racks where current issues of journals and museum bulletins can be displayed with the recent issues stored behind the sloping display shelves.

The staff and user spaces in a very small library must usually be integrated for reasons of security and the provision of service. Architects have a tendency, which must be checked early in the planning process, to design reading rooms with the staff office areas at the end of the library opposite from the entrance. If the library plan does not incorporate an information or charge-out counter at the main entrance, at least one employee desk should be immediately inside the entrance to serve as an inquiry center and to discourage unauthorized borrowing of library materials. The office of the librarian may be further from the entrance, but should have a glass wall overlooking the reading room, to permit surveillance and simplify provision of assistance to users.

The card catalog cabinet and/or computer terminal, as well as shelving for reference materials, will be located in the reading room. The first item of equipment to be added as soon as funding can be found is a photocopier (this can serve the whole museum), followed by a microform viewer or reader-printer. Both new and old libraries have to consider microform purchases today because the costs of out-of-print materials and of reprints added to the cost of prime storage space may rule out other means of collection building. Even small libraries should have a sufficient number of electric outlets and heavy duty lines ready for these machines and other types of equipment because, even if they seem out of reach at present, the speed of technological advance may soon bring them within the limits of the budget. Both museum and library services are being automated and systems networks are being developed. Since such projects often receive funding from outside sources, the small museum may suddenly find it advantageous and within its means to be linked by computer terminals and communication lines to vast data banks of stored knowledge and information, and it should be prepared to do so.

Conclusion

A well thought out plan for facilities within the library is the most important contribution the librarian can make to the development process for the museum building. The plan should be based on the nature of the library's role in fulfilling the policies of the governing institution and its preparation will draw on the librarian's specialized knowledge of the library's needs. It should deal with the location of the library premises, the different library areas and their relationship to each other, and should list in detail the fixtures and services required in each area, and the furniture and equipment most suitable for the various tasks to be performed. Good physical arrangements facilitate good library service.

Additional information beyond the scope of this chapter can be found in the publications listed in the bibliography. Because the books by Michael Brawne, Keyes Metcalf, and Anthony and Godfrey Thompson deal with large separate library buildings, they may not at first glance appear applicable to a library located in a building constructed for a different purpose. However, they are worth studying for the information on the layout and interrelationships of library areas, interior design, furnishings, and equipment.

BIBLIOGRAPHY

Ahrensfeld, Janet L.; Christianson, Elin B.; and King, David E. *Special Libraries: A Guide for Management*. 2d ed. New York: Special Libraries Association, 1982.
American Library Association. Library Administration Division. *Library Furniture and Equipment*. Chicago: American Library Association, 1963.
————. Library Buildings and Equipment Institute. *Planning Library Buildings for Service*. Chicago: American Library Association, 1964.
————. Library Buildings Institute. *Problems in Planning Library Facilities: Consultants, Architects, Plans, and Critiques*. Chicago: American Library Association, 1964.
————. Library Equipment Institute. *The Library Environment: Aspects of Interior Planning*. Chicago: American Library Association, 1965.
————. Library Technology Project. *Protecting the Library and Its Resources: A Guide to Physical Protection and Insurance*. Chicago: American Library Association, 1963.
Bahr, Alice Harrison. *Book Theft and Library Security Systems*. White Plains, N.Y.: Knowledge Industry, 1978.
Brawne, Michael. *Libraries: Architecture and Equipment*. New York: Praeger, 1970.
Cohen, Aaron, and Cohen, Elaine. *Designing and Space Planning for Libraries: A Behavioral Guide*. New York: Bowker, 1979.
Cohen, Elaine, and Cohen, Aaron. *Automation, Space Management, and Productivity: A Guide for Libraries*. New York: Bowker, 1982.

Gandert, Slade Richard. *Protecting Your Collection: A Handbook, Survey, and Guide for the Security of Rare Books, Manuscripts, Archives, and Works of Art.* New York: Haworth, 1980.

Lewis, Chester M. *Special Libraries: How to Plan and Equip Them.* New York: Special Libraries Association, 1963. (SLA Monograph, no. 2).

Library Journal. (Each year the 1 December issue is devoted to library architecture.)

Lushington, Nolan and Willis N. Mills, Jr. AIA. *Libraries Designed for Users.* Hamden, Conn.: Library Professional Publications, 1979.

Lyles, Marjorie Appleman. "Environmental Design Applications." *Special Libraries* 63 (November 1972):495–501.

Mason, Ellsworth D. *Mason on Library Buildings.* Metuchen, N.J.: Scarecrow, 1980.

Metcalf, Keyes. *Planning Academic and Research Library Buildings.* New York: McGraw-Hill, 1965.

Mount, Ellis. *Planning the Special Library.* New York: Special Libraries Association, 1972. (SLA Monograph, no. 4).

Park, Leland M. "The Whys and Hows of Writing a Library Building Program." *Library Scene* 5 (September 1976):2–5.

Public Works Canada. *Departmental Library Facilities.* Ottawa, Ont.: Public Works, 1975. (Briefing Document D-Lib-1).

Rovelstad, Howard. "Guidelines for Planning Facilities for Sci-Tech Libraries," *Science & Technology Libraries* 3 (Summer 1983):3–19.

Somer, Robert. *Tight Spaces: Hard Architecture and How to Humanize It.* Englewood Cliffs, N.J.: Prentice-Hall, 1974.

Special Libraries Association. *Objectives and Standards for Special Libraries.* New York: Special Libraries Association, 1964.

Tactum, Michael. "Trouble-Free Library Planning and Construction." *American Libraries* 1 (October 1970):878–83.

Thompson, Anthony. *Library Buildings of Britain and Europe.* London: Butterworth, 1963.

Thompson, Godfrey. *Planning and Design of Library Buildings.* 2d ed. London: Architectural Press, 1974.

Notes on Contributors

Sylva S. Baker, Head Librarian of the Academy of Natural Sciences in Philadelphia, has directed various cataloging projects for retrospective conversion, overseen inclusion of current serial holdings in the Pennsylvania On-line Union List of Serials, and is supervising creation of a micro-based database for an item-level catalog of 20,000 photographs. She has reorganized Academy library cataloging procedures to be compatible with OCLC network membership. Ms. Baker has received grants from the Strengthening Library Resources Program of the U.S. Department of Education, the State Library of Pennsylvania, and the Dolfinger-McMahon and Staffett Foundations.

M. Noël Balke, Chief Librarian of the National Gallery of Canada until her retirement in 1979, twice redesigned the library for different buildings and organized the removal and relocation of the collections. She was also involved in planning library facilities in the new permanent home for the National Gallery now under construction in Ottawa. Mrs. Balke was a founding member of the Art Libraries Committee of the Canadian Library Association, and has served as Chairman of the Special Libraries Association's Museums, Arts and Humanities Division and Secretary of the Art Libraries Round Table of the International Federation of Library Associations and Institutions.

Minda A. Bojin, Branch Librarian at the National Museum of Science and Technology at the National Museums of Canada, has studied history and political science and has a graduate degree in library science.

Katharine E. S. Donahue, Museum Librarian at the Natural History Museum of Los Angeles County, has established and developed a special collection of Western history materials for the museum. She has supervised the reshelving of the entire library collection and has coordinated the introduction of the OCLC system in her library. Mrs. Donahue is a regular contributor to professional literature.

Julie Diepenbrock Herrick administered the Museum Reference Center, Office of Museum Programs, Smithsonian Institution, after working in the National Collection of Fine Arts/National Portrait Gallery library. She has held professional positions in reader service in federal academic and special libraries, and is presently Public Services Librarian with the U.S. Army in West Germany. Mrs. Herrick has done graduate study in museum and archival administration.

Nina J. Root, Chairwoman of the Department of Library Services at the American Museum of Natural History, has organized the National Preservation Conferences, was the first chairperson of the Preservation of Library Materials Section of the American Library Association's Resources and Technical Services Division, and is currently a member of the Council of the American Library Association and the library advisory council of the New York State Board of Regents. A lecturer in the American Museum of Natural History lecture series and a frequent speaker at professional meetings, Ms. Root is the American representative of the Society for the History of Natural History.

Leslie H. Tepper, an organizer of children's workshops, and special needs and outreach programs for the National Museum of Man, a division of the National Museum of Canada, has a graduate degree in anthropology and a diploma in museum studies.

Enid T. Thompson, Director of Archival Studies at the University of Denver, was formerly Head of the Library at the Colorado Historical Society. Mrs. Thompson is the author of numerous articles and books, including *Local History Collections*, published by the American Association for State and Local History.

Juanita Toupin, Librarian at the Montreal Museum of Fine Arts, has been the recipient of provincial and federal research grants as well as grants from the Social Sciences and Humanities Research Council of Canada and the National Museums of Canada. Miss Toupin has recently been involved in two major research projects dealing with materials in the Montreal Museum of Fine Arts: the *Index to 19th Century Newspaper Clippings* and the *Répertoire numérique detaillé des archives 1860–1976.*

Elizabeth Reuter Usher, Chief Librarian of the Thomas J. Watson Library of the Metropolitan Museum of Art until her retirement in 1980, (when she was elected Chief Librarian Emeritus), has served as president of the Special Libraries Association, member of the Standards Committee of the Art Libraries Society of North America, and trustee of the New York Metropolitan Reference and Research Library Agency. Named to the SLA Hall of Fame, Mrs. Usher continues to be active in the library world through contributions to professional literature.

William B. Walker, Arthur K. Watson Chief Librarian of the Thomas J. Watson Library at the Metropolitan Museum of Art, is currently a member of the Art Section Standing Committee of the International Federation of Library Associations and Institutions. Mr. Walker is active in professional library associations and has been a consultant to various art agencies, including the Archives of American Art.

Index